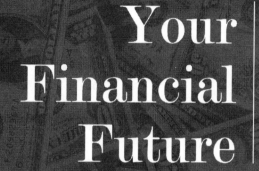

Your Financial Future

A
Guide
to Life
After
Graduation

1st Edition

A Life After Graduation, LLC Publication
5645 Kathryn Street • Alexandria, Virginia • 22303
(877) 569-9816 • www.LifeAfterGraduation.com

COPYRIGHT INFORMATION

BOOK DISCLAIMER

Your Financial Future

Table of Contents

Introduction **15**

Chapter 1:
Your Financial Goals **18**
- Defining Your Goals
- Prioritizing Your Goals
- Assigning Values To Your Goals
- Implementing Your Plan

Chapter 2:
Budgeting **22**
- How Much Money Is Coming In?
- How Much Money Is Going Out?
- Is There Enough?
- Keep At It

Chapter 3:
Net Worth **30**
- What Are Your Assets?
- What Are Your Liabilities?
- What Is Your Net Worth?

Chapter 4:
Debt Management **33**
- Debt Warning Signs
- Good Debt vs. Bad Debt
- How Much Debt Do You Have?
- What Is An Acceptable Level Of Debt?

- Paying Off Your Debt
- If You Have Too Much Debt
- Collection Agencies
- Bankruptcy

Chapter 5:
Credit Cards 42
- The Value Of Credit Cards
- Credit Cards – What You Need To Know And Do
- What Is Worse – Annual Fees Or Interest Rates?
- Comparing Credit Cards
- Credit Card Fraud

Chapter 6:
Student Loans 51
- What Type Of Loan(s) Do You Have?
- Understanding Your Loan(s)
- Loan Consolidation
- Deferment And Forbearance
- Forgiveness Of Loans
- Discounts
- Tax Benefits
- Defaulting On Your Student Loan
- Bankruptcy And Student Loans

Chapter 7:
Credit Reports 57
- Credit Report & Credit Score – What Are They?
- What Does A Credit Report Say About You?

- Who Has The Right To See Your Credit Report?
- When Should You Get A Copy Of Your Credit Report?
- How Do You Get A Copy Of Your Credit Report?
- How Do You Fix Mistakes In Your Credit Report?
- What If You're Denied Credit?
- What If You Have Bad Credit?

Chapter 8:
Identity Theft 63
- How Does Identity Theft Occur?
- What Thieves Do With Your Information
- How Can You Minimize Your Risk?
- Protecting Yourself On The Web
- What To Do If You Are The Victim Of Identity Theft

Chapter 9:
Banking 68
- Common Banking Mistakes People Make
- Banks – What Are Your Options?
- Choosing A Bank
- Comparison-Shopping
- Free Checking – Is It Really Free?
- Avoiding Banking Fees

- On Line Banking
- Managing Your Account
- Store Your Records
- Balance Your Account Each Month

Chapter 10:
Insurance. 78
- What Should You Insure?
- Shopping For The Right Insurance Provider
- Take Advantage Of Employer-Provided Insurance
- Auto Insurance
- Health Insurance
- Life Insurance
- Homeowner's Insurance
- Renter's Insurance
- Disability Insurance
- Reducing The Cost Of Insurance
- Insurance You Don't Need

Chapter 11:
Housing: Rent vs. Buy. 99
- Rent Or Buy – Which Is Better For You?
- The Smart Renter
- What Does A Home Cost?
- Mortgage Options
- Special Programs For New Homebuyers
- The Home Buying Process

Chapter 12:
Car: Lease vs. Buy. 112
- Can You Afford A New Car?
- Determining The Car You Need
- Should You Buy New Or Used?
- Should You Lease Or Buy?
- What About Your Current Car?
- Preparing For The Test Drive
- How To Test Drive A Car
- Determining The Price
- Financing Your Purchase
- Choosing The Car For You
- Purchasing Your Car

Chapter 13:
Investing 123
- Saving vs. Investing
- A Word On Inflation
- Are You Ready To Start Investing?
- What Do You Need To Start Investing?
- How Much Risk Can You Tolerate?
- When Do You Want To Use Your Investments?
- What Are Your Investment Options?
- Diversification
- Asset Allocation
- Which Investments Should You Choose?

- Where Should You Purchase Your Investments?

Chapter 14:
Retirement **134**
- How Much Money Do You Need To Retire?
- Defined-Benefit vs. Employer-Sponsored Plans
- Employer-Sponsored Plans
- Changing Jobs
- Self-Employed And Small Business Plans
- Individual Retirement Accounts (IRAs)
- Social Security
- Seven Steps To A Successful Retirement Program

Chapter 15:
Financial Planners **145**
- What Makes Someone A Good Financial "Coach?"
- How Do Financial Planners Earn A Living?
- Where Can You Find A Financial Coach?
- Interviewing A Prospective Coach
- What About Certifications?
- Things Your Financial Planner Should Never Do

Chapter 16:
Home Equity **150**
- Home Equity Loan vs. Line Of Credit

- What Can Home Equity Be Used For?
- Is Using Home Equity Right For You?
- The 125 Percent Home Equity Loan

Chapter 17:
Taxes **156**
- Understanding Taxes
- How Is Your Income Tax Calculated?
- Marginal & Effective Tax Rates
- Reporting Your Taxes
- Reducing Your Tax Burden
- Keeping Records
- Tax Assistance
- Rapid Refund Offers

Chapter 18:
Estate Planning **167**
- What Is Estate Planning?
- What Is A Will?
- Medical Directive (aka: Living Will)
- Probate And Trusts
- Estate Taxes
- Do You Need An Attorney?
- Funeral Arrangements

DEDICATION

This book is dedicated to you—the recent graduate. We hope this book provides you with the tools and resources that will allow you to make informed and educated financial decisions. Decisions that will provide you the financial success you deserve.

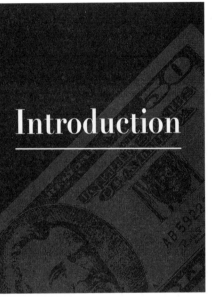

Introduction

First things first. Congratulations! Whether you just graduated from college or have been in the "real world" for a while, you've done yourself a huge favor by reading Your Financial Future. Why? Because you're about to accomplish something most Americans haven't – financial literacy.

You've spent your entire life preparing for your future. However, if you're like most recent graduates, there is one subject you have failed to prepare for – managing your personal finances.

Personal finance is one of the most important subjects we never learn about – except in the school of hard knocks called experience. And then the lessons are often very hard ones. They include incurring too much debt, failing to save, and ultimately having no way to work out of a financial hole if something unforeseen happens in your life.

Your degree has prepared you for a career. No one has prepared you for life's pitfalls like lack of planning, wasteful spending, procrastination, failure to do sufficient research before you make important financial decisions, and on and on. You're turned loose on the world unarmed and uninformed.

Consider these facts:
- Americans today have a long life expectancy, but little job security and few benefits.
- The average annual personal savings rates for Americans are a paltry 3 to 5 percent of household income.
- Our desire for immediate gratification and exorbitant spending has created a society dependent on credit cards and other forms of high-interest debt.

- On top of mounting student loans, the average college student graduates with a credit card debt of $3,000.

- 1.5 million Americans will declare bankruptcy this year. One-third of these people are in their 20s and 30s.

- Most Americans spend more time planning their one-week summer vacation than their 30-year retirement.

- Only 5 percent of people over 65 years of age have a yearly income over $40,000.

- To have $1 million for retirement, you will need to save $300 a month for 30 years in an account averaging a return of 10 percent. Most financial experts say retirees need at least $2 million to retire comfortably.

- Based on 2005 expenses, you'll need $260,000 to send your first child to a four-year college in 2025 and $285,000 to send your second in 2030.

Are you prepared to manage your personal finances? You will be after reading Your Financial Future.

Your Financial Future is organized in bite-sized chapters to give you the basics on things like getting the best deal on a new car, finding the best bank, managing credit, and what kinds of insurance you need. You'll establish your tolerance for financial risk and learn about investing versus saving. You'll find tips on buying a home, setting goals, and managing a budget. There are answers to questions about confusing topics like taxes, estates, and retirement.

Your Financial Future will make you literate, financially speaking. Financial literacy means knowing how to sort through the complex world of personal finance. It means knowing the vocabulary required to manage your personal finances successfully. It means not falling prey to obstacles like too many choices, lack of time, or the biggest obstacle of all: not knowing what to do. Being financially literate means you will feel competent instead of overwhelmed when faced with financial decisions, clear instead of confused when presented with choices, and confident instead of frightened about financial matters.

Your Financial Future will give you a sufficient foundation to control your personal finances, shed light on some very important subjects, and provide the tools and resources you need to become an effective manager of your personal finances.

A little time and energy spent on managing your personal finances now will reap you large rewards in the future. Don't wait. **Your Financial Future starts right here, right now!**

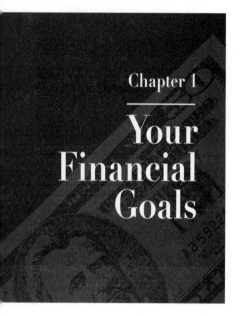

Chapter 1

Your Financial Goals

Everyone has goals. They may be short-term *(I need to rent an apartment)* or long-term *(I'm going to retire before I'm 50!)*, but most people never write them down. Everyone talks about what they want, but never bother to figure out how to get it. In addition, most people never sit down with a pencil and piece of paper, write down their goals, and then figure out how to go after them and make them real.

All successful companies have a business plan that carefully outlines what tasks must be done to achieve desired financial goals. This chapter will help you do the exact same thing.

Defining Your Goals

Grab a pad of paper and pencil. You might want a cup of coffee, or a can of soda as well. Find a quiet place and spend some time thinking about what you want to accomplish in your life. Make a list of all the things you want to do – travel, buy a house, buy a car, get married – whatever these goals and dreams are, write them down even if they sound silly or impossible.

Some things that might appear on your list:

- Pay off my student loans
- Get out of debt
- Create an emergency cash fund
- Travel
- Buy a car
- Exercise more
- Find the perfect life partner

Not a bad list, but it could use more detail. Take "travel," for instance. Where do you want to go? For example, taking an annual weekend trip to Las Vegas to hang out with your college friends counts as travel. The more specifically you define your goals, the easier the next steps will be.

Also, be very honest with yourself when you create your list. Remember, you don't need to share it with anyone. These goals need to be your goals, not your father's or your best friend's – yours and yours alone.

Now, sort your goals into two lists – one for goals that cost money, and one for everything else. Don't abandon the non-financial goals. After all, finding the perfect life partner would definitely be very rewarding. But this book is focused on your financial future – something over which you have some control – so let's discuss the goals that cost money.

Prioritizing Your Goals

By now you've got quite a list, and it can be overwhelming. How in the world will you be able to accomplish all this in one lifetime? By prioritizing. There's an old adage that you can't eat an elephant in one sitting. Well, you can't accomplish all your goals at once either.

Take your list of finance-related goals and pick the most important on the list. Maybe it's to buy a new car. If you have debt, consider making "get out of debt" your most important goal, as debt can make reaching your other goals very challenging.

Begin a new list, this time with your goals listed in order of importance. As you work through the list, you may decide that some of the things you came up with the first time through aren't as important any more. Fine – drop them. Or you may think up other goals. Also fine. Add them in order of importance to your new list.

As you prioritize your list, you may realize that some of your goals are not well defined. For instance, "I want to be wealthy" is an admirable goal, but wealth means different things to different people. For you, "wealthy" may mean having a million dollars, while for someone else, $50 million is the minimum threshold of "wealthy." Not to worry. The next section will help you define your goals.

Assigning Values To Your Goals

All goals, in order to be reached, should share these characteristics:

- They should be measurable

- They should have a timetable
- They should involve a strategy

Back to your prioritized list. Read through it carefully and then transfer it to the following chart, filling in the missing parts.

My Goals

Goal	Money Needed to Achieve Goal	Strategy to Reach Goal	Date to Achieve Goal
Pay off student loans	$12,000	• Consolidate loans • Make payments. on time • Make extra payment of $300/month	12/31/2010
1.			
2.			
3.			
4.			

Take as much time and paper as you need. Get another cup of coffee or can of soda. What you're building is a plan for your financial future, and it deserves your best effort and best ideas.

Your goals will change over time, and you will want to review this list at least annually. First, because you will have met some goals each year. And second, because you'll develop more goals as you go through life.

So now you've got your list prioritized, you've assigned values and strategies, and the timeframe for reaching each goal. Now what?

Implementing Your Plan

Obviously, money is the key to reaching your goals and you *(probably)* don't have an unlimited supply of greenbacks. Right? Therefore, you need a budget. As you will learn in the next chapter, a budget is an important tool that will help you reach your goals. With a budget, you will develop a list of your day-to-day expenses. You will then subtract the total of these expenses from the amount of income you have and, hopefully, you'll have excess cash. This is the amount you have to work with to reach your goals.

If you thought you'd have and extra $500 each month to use to reach your goals, but you only have $250, then you'll need to adjust your strategy for reaching your goals. But don't abandon your goals just because meeting them will take a little longer. Simply adjust your goals chart accordingly and you'll get there eventually.

If you want to reach your goals faster, then consult your budget to see if there are expenses you can reduce. Do you really need to eat out every night of the week? How about learning how to make your own meals?

The money you earn is yours to manage as you see fit. Goals and budgets are simply tools to help you make informed decisions on how to manage that money. In addition, there are other tools presented in this book that will help you reach your goals. Realize that your financial picture will change over time, so don't put that list of goals too far away. Check it at least annually to see how far you've come toward reaching your goals. You'll be amazed at how well it works – and how good it feels once you begin to accomplish them.

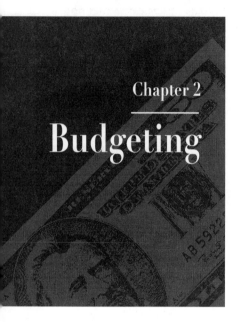

Chapter 2

Budgeting

The more money we make, the more we spend. Isn't that the truth? Think about it. If you lived like you did during college, but had the income you're earning now, how much extra money would you have to reach the goals you outlined in the previous chapter? This doesn't mean you should go back to living a life fueled by ramen noodles and mac and cheese. It means that you now have more income than you had during college, and you should take appropriate steps to make the most of that income. And that means creating a budget.

Yes, budgets conjure up images of doing without – and it isn't in the nature of most Americans to want to wait for anything. We are the most marketed-to people on the planet, and those marketing messages tell us to consume, consume, consume. Curbing the impulse to buy whatever we want when we want is tough. But if you want to achieve your financial goals, you have to pay attention to where your money is going. And the single – best tool to help you do that is a budget.

It will take some time to create a good budget, but you'll have made a great accomplishment when you're done. Budgets not only tell you where your money is going, they help you set goals. With a budget you'll be able to better manage your time and your money.

How Much Money Is Coming In?

In order to manage the money you're paying out, you need to know how much you have coming in. It's important to identify all the sources of income you have: your paycheck, interest on checking and savings accounts, gifts from mom and dad. List it all. You can use the following chart as a starting place.

Monthly Income

Source of Income	Amount Per Month
Gross Salary (before taxes/deductions)	$1,545
Part-time job	$575
Interest from savings	$35
TOTAL	
Average/Month	

How Much Money Is Going Out?

The only way to know how much money you're paying out is to list everything you spend money on. So get a pad of paper and start writing. Here are some of the more common categories of expenses:

- **Housing** – Whether you rent or pay a mortgage, this is probably the largest expense on your list. If you're still living at home, perhaps you're contributing some money to your parents.

- **Utilities** – All the things we take for granted, like electricity, water, gas, phone, and garbage collection fall into this category. Gather up receipts you've paid over the past few months and you'll have a good idea of how much these expenses cost.

- **Debts** – Probably the second-largest category in your list of expenses is repayment of debts. Include payments on everything for which you owe money: student loans, car payments, credit cards, etc.

- **Insurance** – Auto, health, renter's or homeowner's – include all the insurance you pay for.

- **Taxes** – Analyze your paycheck and any other documents that identify the amount of taxes you pay. Includes items like state, federal, Social Security and Medicare taxes. You may find it helpful to review your past state and federal income tax returns and calculate a monthly total to determine if you are contributing the correct amount to your tax bill each month.

- **Transportation** – This includes all expenses to keep your car working, like gas, oil changes and repairs. In addition, include in this category items like tolls, licensing/registration fees, and vehicle inspections. If you routinely use public transportation like the bus or subway, include that amount in this category.

- **Entertainment** – This may be another big category. Include everything you do for fun – movies, vacations, eating out *(yes, include those Big Macs)*, concerts, Internet access, the double latte you have every morning, the clubs you go to on weekends. Everything. Don't forget books, CDs, DVDs *(either bought or rented)*, and cable TV. If the expenses in this category are quite large, you might consider breaking it up into smaller categories like "Eating Out" and "Vacations."

- **Personal** – Food, clothing, shoes, dry cleaning, health club fees, haircuts, manicures, make-up, pet care – expenses like these make up this category.

- **Contributions** – List any money you contribute to charities or other organizations.

- **Retirement/Savings** – Hopefully you are contributing to your employer's retirement program or some other form of retirement/ savings program. If so, add these amounts to your budget.

You may be able to think of even more categories. List them. Leave nothing out.

Once you have a complete list of your expenses, break them up into fixed and variable expenses.

Fixed Expenses

Fixed expenses occur regularly and generally in the same amount – like rent. Sometimes fixed expenses occur every month *(rent, fitness club dues)*, but some happen annually or quarterly, like car insurance. Because they happen regularly and the amounts don't change, it should be easy to list your fixed expenses. Checks you've written should be listed in your check register – you can get the amounts from there. Or gather up the receipts from the last few months' bills and take the numbers from there. The following charts will help you organize your monthly and yearly fixed expenses. Assign your monthly expenses to the appropriate day of the month on which they normally occur. Assign your yearly expenses to the month of the year they occur.

Monthly Fixed Expenses

1 Ex: Rent $550	12	23
2	13	24
3	14	25
4	15 Ex: Cable $45	26
5	16	27
6	17	28
7	18	29
8	19	30
9 Insurance: $98	20	31
10	21	
11	22	Monthly Total:

Yearly Fixed Expense

JANUARY	
FEBRUARY	
MARCH	Ex. Car Registration $380
APRIL	
MAY	
JUNE	
JULY	
AUGUST	
SEPTEMBER	
OCTOBER	
NOVEMBER	
DECEMBER	Ex. Holiday Gifts $200
TOTAL	
Monthly Average	

Variable Expenses

After you've identified all your fixed expenses, list your variable expenses. As the name suggests, these expenses vary in both amount and frequency.

Groceries, entertainment, gasoline and long-distance phone calls all fall into this category.

Because they change, variable expenses are a little more difficult to determine. Many people simply estimate them, but avoid the temptation to do this because most people greatly underestimate the amount they spend on variable items. You need to be as accurate as possible, because you can't meet your goals with guesses.

Here's a surefire way to nail down what you're spending: write down every penny you spend for a month. Don't moan. Simply carry a small notebook with you or enter the cost of that morning coffee in your PDA. You'll be astonished at where your spare cash goes. But that knowledge will be invaluable in helping you manage your money. Other things you can do include:

- Write a description of the purchase for each check you write.
- Keep all receipts from credit card purchases and write the purpose of the expense on the back of the receipt.
- Record your daily spending in a spreadsheet or on a chart.
- Once a week, review your daily expenses and total them. The results are likely to be a big surprise!

After you've collected a month's worth of variable expenses, you should be in a better position to determine how much you spend for each kind of variable expense. If you want to be even more accurate, continue collecting daily spending records for another two months.

The following chart is an example of how you can record your variable expenses. You will notice that there is a section for credit card expenses – use it only if you are currently paying off previous credit card balances. If you purchase items during the month with your credit card that would be classified as variable expenses, list those in the appropriate category. For example, if you purchase $40 worth of groceries with your credit card, enter that amount in the "Groceries" section.

Monthly Variable Expenses

Expenses	Wk 1	Wk 2	Wk 3	Wk 4	TOTALS
Automobile					
Household					
Snacks					

Monthly Variable Expenses Continued

Entertainment					
Laundry					
Groceries					
Personal Care					
Utilities					
Credit Card					
Other:					
TOTALS					

Recycle this chart as many times as you want – and change the expense categories to fit your circumstances – but be sure to keep track of everything you spend money on for at least a month.

Is There Enough?

Now that you have completed the income, fixed expense and variable expense charts, you have the ingredients that make up a budget. At this point, completing your budget is fairly simple. Simply transfer your carefully gathered information into the following chart, called an Income Statement:

Income Statement

Monthly Income	
Minus Monthly Fixed Expenses	
Minus Yearly Fixed Expenses (Monthly Average)	
Minus Monthly Variable Expenses	
Remaining Income	

More Expenses Than Income

If the number in the Remaining Income box is negative, you are spending more money than you earn every month. As deflating as this realization may be, it can be fixed. One solution is to earn more money, but you may not have control over this. A far more direct solution is to spend less.

Don't groan. Look again at your variable expenses and mark those that could be reduced. Perhaps you eat out two or three times a week. Try eating at home instead. Be honest and ruthless in cutting variable expenses. Spending more than you earn is a path to failure.

And don't let your fixed expenses escape scrutiny. Think creatively. Maybe you need a roommate to split your rent. Or perhaps you need to move to a less expensive, smaller apartment. If you're paying a mortgage, look into refinancing. If interest rates have come down since you bought your house, you could end up paying less each month. That fitness club you're paying dues for each month? Be honest. Do you really use it? Or could you get fit by running the track at the local high school?

Once you've identified all the ways you can reduce your expenses, redo your budget. Did you change enough things to have a positive number in your remaining income? If not, continue to evaluate steps you can take to reduce your spending. Keep in mind that just breaking even is not enough. For example, what happens when those unexpected yet inevitable expenses show up – like a car accident, or your computer dies? Unexpected expenses make it imperative that your remaining income number is positive.

More Income Than Expenses

If the number in the bottom, right-hand box is positive, congratulations! You are living within your means – spending less than you take in. This is a very good position to be in. Pat yourself on the back and be proud of your accomplishments.

Now go get that list of financial goals you put together and see how far your extra money will go toward achieving those goals. For example, if one of your short-term goals is to pay off your student loans and you have $100 leftover each month, you can now determine how long it will take you to accumulate enough money to fulfill that goal.

Keep in mind that as you pay down your debts (*this should be one of your top goals*) you'll have even more discretionary income – money not tagged for fixed or variable expenses – and will more easily be able to achieve your financial goals.

Keep At It

Once you have developed a budget, don't let all your hard work go to waste. This wasn't a one-time activity, but an important part of your overall financial routine. Any time something changes in your life – you get a better job or you decide to get married – you should reevaluate your budget. And it's actually a good idea to look at your budget every few months, even if there haven't been any major changes in your life.

If you're computer savvy, there are a lot of software programs out there to help you establish and maintain a budget. Microsoft Money and Quicken offer perhaps the most recognized and helpful programs. In addition, there are a number of Web sites that offer advice on budgeting.

While all these tools may make budgeting jazzier, remember that all you really need is the determination to make your budget and stick to it.

Chapter 3

Net Worth

Your net worth can be determined simply by subtracting your liabilities *(money you owe)* from the value of your assets *(things you own)*. The result is your net worth. While net worth is just a number, it has some useful purposes. For example, it can help you acquire a loan, as well as plan for your future.

If you're like most recent college graduates, your net worth is probably negative. But don't worry, that will change. The important thing to know right now is how to calculate your net worth and evaluate the results.

If you've created a budget, have that handy because it can help make determining your net worth easier. So pick up that calculator and get ready to figure out your net worth.

What Are Your Assets?

Assets are things you own, like a car or your computer. They're also things like bank accounts, bonds, stocks, and mutual funds. Take a look at the following chart, then gather your financial records and fill it out. Add everything up, and that number represents your total assets.

Assets

Description of Assets	Estimated Value
Cash – Checking & Savings Accts.	$8,500
Money people owe you	$0
Stocks, bonds & mutual funds	$13,500
Life Insurance *(cash value)*	$0
IRA accounts	$2,500

Assets Contiued

401(k) accounts *(vested amounts)*	$3,500
Real Estate	
Home	$0
Other	$0
Personal property *(car, furniture, jewelry, collections, antiques, security or rent deposits, etc.)*	$25,000
TOTAL	**$53,000**

That wasn't bad, was it? Be sure you include everything in your list and then go on to liabilities.

What Are Your Liabilities?

Assets are what you own, and liabilities are what you owe – both short term and long term. These include student loans, mortgages (both are long-term liabilities), as well as your current credit card bills, taxes, and current bills for things like electricity and water.

Take a look at the following chart. You'll see the format is similar to how you determined your assets.

Liabilities

Description of Liability	Estimated Value
Mortgage	$0
Rent *(For the year)*	$9,000
Bank loans	$0
Car loan	$4,500
Lines of credit	$500
Credit card balances	$5,250
Student loans	$32,000
Other liabilities	$0
TOTAL	**$51,250**

If you've managed your money well up to now, your total assets should outweigh your liabilities. And that's where net worth comes in.

What Is Your Net Worth?

Net worth is the difference between your total assets and your total liabilities. Using the two examples above, the net worth of our Example Person is figured like this:

Total Assets	**$53,000**
-Total Liabilities	**$51,250**
=Net Worth	**$ 1,750**

If your calculation results in a negative number – and it may, depending on how long you've been out of college – don't panic. A net worth calculation is simply a snapshot of where you are financially at any given time. Do the net worth calculation six months from now, and it will have changed because your financial picture will have changed.

Why bother with this exercise, you might ask. Because it can help you set financial goals, help you judge your progress towards those goals, and make financial decisions. If you're planning on buying a home, your mortgage lender will need to know your net worth. So if you've already computed it, you're a step ahead.

And if your net worth is a negative number, it reminds you to get your financial affairs in order so your net worth will be positive the next time you calculate it.

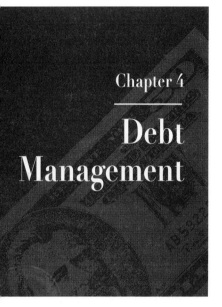

Chapter 4

Debt Management

Like most college graduates, you have a dream of life after graduation that includes making a lot of money and living the good life. Unfortunately, for most college graduates this dream is diminished by the large amount of debt they have accrued during their heydays at college.

The fact is, most college graduates have large amounts of student loans, multiple credit card balances, and a variety of other forms of debt. And, as you know, all of these need to be paid.

But don't give up on your dream of the good life just yet. There is hope. However, it's up to you to make it happen. So how do you make it happen? By putting your debt into perspective and developing a plan to get yourself out of debt as soon as possible.

Debt Warning Signs

The first step to putting your debt into perspective is to recognize when your debt is a problem. Monitor your debt every month and watch for any of these red flags:

- Living from paycheck to paycheck with nothing leftover at the end of each month.
- Impulse buying. Did you absolutely have to have those new shoes, that 52-inch HDTV, or that new computer?
- Making late or minimum monthly payments on your credit card(s), or skipping payments altogether.
- Having credit cards that are at, or close to, your credit limit.
- Arguing with family members or friends over your spending habits.
- Being unsure of how much you really owe.

- Using cash advances to pay your bills.
- Having more and more of your monthly income that must go to paying off your debts.
- Having your credit card declined, or being turned down for additional credit.

Do you recognize yourself in any of these scenarios? If so, it's time you develop a plan to get out of debt.

Good Debt vs. Bad Debt

As you begin creating a get-out-of-debt game plan, you must first understand what kind of debt you have. There are two types: good debt and bad debt. Your goal is to rid yourself of your bad debts first.

So what is the difference between good and bad debt? It's pretty simple: Good debt is debt that returns something of long term value to you, such as higher education, or home improvements that increase the value of your home. Bad debt can often be categorized as short-term "feel good" debt, like unwise purchases you can't afford and don't really need.

How Much Debt Do You Have?

Now is the time for the reality check. Sit down with paper, pencil and a calculator and start by making a list of all – and we mean all – of your debts. By each of your debts, indicate whether the debt is a good or bad debt. Next, rank them in descending order by their interest rates.

Now, organize your debts. Here is a form you can use:

Good Debts

Name of Loan	Principal Owed	Interest Rate	Annual Interest Payment (Est.)
Mortgage	$96,552	6.75%	$96,552 x 0.0675 = $6,517
Student Loan	$27,000	4.50%	$27,000 x 0.0450 = $1,215
TOTAL			

Bad Debts

Name of Loan	Principal Owed	Interest Rate	Annual Interest Payment (Est.)
Visa	$5,522	15.75%	$5,522 x 0.1575 = $870
Gas Card	$648	11.25%	$648 x 1.1125 = $73
TOTAL			

What Is An Acceptable Level Of Debt?

If your bad debt column is blank, and if you have been truthful, give yourself a pat on the back and keep on doing what you've been doing. But if you've got entries in the "bad" column, it's time to do some calculations.

Add up the total amount of interest paid on bad debt. Now, add up the total principle you owe. Figure out your total annual income after taxes. Now make a ratio out of these two numbers.

Using the previous example the ratio looks like this:

Total Bad Debt:	**$6,173**
Total Annual Income, After Taxes:	**$32,000**
Bad Debt-to-Income Ratio:	**$6,173/$32,000 = 19.3%**

As a general rule, anything over 15 percent should sound an alarm and get you motivated to lower it as soon as possible. The goal is to get your bad debt as close to zero as you can, in as short a time as possible.

You may be wondering why good debt is not included in this equation. Good debt helps your overall financial posture. Of course, if you've gone out on a limb with your home purchase, or your student loans are staggering, you may wish to include those numbers in your bad debt equation.

Paying Off Your Debt

Take a good look at your bad debt chart, focusing on the balance with the highest interest rate. This is your starting point. Start your get out of debt plan by paying that one off first. Once you've paid off your most costly debt, don't stop there. Move on to the next one, and pay that off. Work your way down the chart until you have eliminated all your bad debt.

Right now you are probably thinking, "sure, that seems simple enough, but how on earth am I going to find the money to start paying down this bad debt? Here's how:

- **Lose the credit cards** – Put them in a safe, hide them – or even better, cut them up. Start spending cash or use a debit card. That way you can't spend what you don't have.

- **Develop a budget** – Do it with thorough charts, in writing. Study your spending habits, your obligations, and the places where you are most likely to get in trouble. Be sure that your written budget prioritizes the paying down of your bad debt first, but also make sure you can pay down your good debts on schedule, as required. Never let these slide.

- **Live within your means** – Stop all impulse buying, and don't lie to yourself about this. Iron your own shirts. Brown bag your lunch. See the movie when you can rent it for less than half what the theater charges. Shop at thrift shops. Use coupons. Buy only sale items. Eat in, not out. If you're feeling deprived, remind yourself that this is all about your future, maybe even your survival.

- **Pay more than the minimum due each month** – This is a trap set by the bank to own you for eternity. Pay as much as you can stand each month, and then add a few dollars to that. Watch that debt dwindle and congratulate yourself every month.

- **Transfer credit card debt to a low interest card** – If you have too much debt to put onto that card, pay the minimum due on all cards but the worst, and start making as large a monthly payment as you can on that one. It gets easier and easier and feels better and better. Any debts that you can roll into a single debt at a lower interest rate will put money back in your pocket that you can then use to pay down the new, consolidated debt. But be sure to pay very close attention to the fine print involved with these cards, and familiarize yourself with the terms. Understand both the introductory interest rate, as well as what it can grow to and under what circumstances. Many Web sites offer information to help you compare various credit cards to get the best deal. Start with www.bankrate.com or www.cardtrak.com.

- **Refinance your mortgage** – If rates have gone down, consider refinancing. See the Housing: Rent vs. Buy chapter for more information on how to do this.

- **Consolidate student loans** – See the Student Loans chapter for more information on how to do this.

- **Use your savings** – As painful as it is, it makes no sense to let savings sit there and earn a piddling amount of interest (*which is taxable*) when you're paying a much higher interest rate on debt. Paying down your debt technically puts more money in your pocket in the form of interest you no longer have to pay, untaxed, than you can earn on most any savings account.

- **Sell stuff you don't need** – Have a yard sale or sell stuff online. Likewise, if you are driving an expensive car, sell it and replace it with an economy model or, better yet, if you live in an urban area with good public transportation, go carless for a while and see what you save on repairs, insurance and gasoline. Yes, your pride will suffer, but it will suffer worse when you're in bankruptcy court.

- **Use your home's equity** – Review the Home Equity chapter to learn how your home's equity can help you get out of debt.

- **Get a part-time job** – It'll give you a bit of cash to work with and, more to the point, show you that you never want to get into this situation again!

- **Renegotiate with your lenders** – Most lenders will work with you, particularly if your next choice is bankruptcy. Ask for forgiveness on fees, a lower interest rate, and/or a longer repayment schedule.

- **Borrow from your retirement** – "Borrowing" is the important word. And notice that this is listed last. That's because this is not an ideal solution, and should only be considered as a last resort. Before you proceed with this option, consult a professional financial planner. Understand that you are borrowing it from your future, and that you won't have much of a future if you drown in debt before you get there. The terms usually make this an attractive option, because as you pay back the 401(k) plan, the interest you're paying on that loan is being paid to you. But be sure you understand the consequences of this decision. For example, if you decide to leave your job, you must repay the loan within 60 days or you will be subject to various penalties and taxes.

If You Have Too Much Debt

If your situation is beyond the fixes described in the previous section, there are resources to help you.

Financial Advisors

Contact your financial planner, if you have one. He or she can be an excellent source of advice. After all, part of their job is to discuss any financial problems you may have, and too much debt certainly qualifies.

Consumer Credit Counseling Service (CCCS)

If you want to re-negotiate terms with your creditors, you can get free information from the CCCS. Call 800-388-2227 to find an office near you. They will give you general budgeting advice for free, and specific counseling for a low fee.

Keep in mind that CCCS, although marketed as a non-profit organization, is funded in large part (*85 percent*) by fees paid to it by credit card companies in the form of commissions based on collections. This more or less makes CCCS a glorified collection agency, which means it puts the creditor's interest ahead of the debtor's. For example:

- CCCS is unlikely to recommend or even discuss bankruptcy, except to highlight the drawbacks.

- They will put you on a "debt management program" which will require you to pay them a certain sum every month that they, in turn, dole out to your creditors.

- This program favors the repaying of credit card debt and ignores other important debt, like your mortgage and medical bills, from which they get no commission.

- They might suggest that you liquidate your retirement fund, and will not tell you that if you declare bankruptcy, you get to keep your retirement fund.

- CCCS has a cookie-cutter approach to debt management, and will not do much as far as weighing individual circumstances.

- They won't mention that restructuring your credit card debt under their program will have a negative impact on your credit report.

Credit Counselors

Another option is credit counseling groups or credit repair clinics that will work with you for a fee. Be wary of the crooks out there that will take your money and do nothing for you. Be particularly leery of those that promise to "fix your problem fast," get you a "new credit identity," or want their fee up front. Also, beware if they promise to get the bad info off your credit report. Bankruptcies, tax liens, judgments and delinquent payments cannot be removed by anyone for any reason.

Investigate any credit counselor you are considering using with the Better Business Bureau www.bbb.org and any other consumer watchdog group. Other useful websites include:

- www.debtproofliving.com
- The Motley Fool www.Fool.com
- The National Foundation for Consumer Credit www.nfcc.org or 800-388-2227
- Federal Trade Commission www.ftc.gov or 877-FTC-HELP

Collection Agencies

If one or more of your creditors has turned a collection agency on you, know your rights.

- A collection agency may contact you by phone, e-mail, fax, mail, or in person.
- They cannot call you before 8:00 a.m. or after 9:00 p.m.
- They cannot call your boss or members of your family.
- No one else can be forced to pay a debt that is yours alone.
- You can get them to stop calling you by sending them a letter. They are then only allowed to contact you regarding plans to bring legal action against you.

You do not need to tolerate rude or belittling remarks. But by the same token, do not take that same attitude with the collection agency. After all, you do owe the money.

Collection agencies are not empowered to work out payment terms. They make money by collecting a percentage of the amount owed, so they will not cut deals on anything other than, perhaps, payment timetables. If you think you are being treated unfairly, contact the FTC at 877-FTC-HELP and ask for information on the Fair Debt Collection Practices Act, or visit their Web site at www.ftc.gov.

Bankruptcy

Filing for bankruptcy should only be done as a last resort. No one loves it, and you should not go into it casually. However, sometimes it's the only course of action left. There are two forms of personal bankruptcy:

- **Chapter 7 Bankruptcy** – will permit you to discharge certain debts.
- **Chapter 13 Bankruptcy** – will give you a debt repayment schedule. It does not discharge debts, but it does make creditors back off.

There are some drawbacks to filing bankruptcy, and you should clearly understand these before taking such a drastic step:

- Bankruptcy will appear prominently on your credit reports for 10 years after you file for it. This means getting more credit will be difficult, particularly for the first few years.

- You are unlikely to be allowed to make a major purchase, such as a home, in the first five to seven years following the filing. Use that time to build up a down payment for a home purchase. Seven years isn't forever. And as a renter, you won't be paying property taxes or spending your money on home maintenance.

- Filing for bankruptcy costs money. It will probably run you some $1,000 or even more in filing and legal fees.

- Although there is a great emotional benefit to cleaning your slate and starting over, there is stress and some embarrassment that surrounds filing for bankruptcy. It is also unpleasant to have to bare your personal affairs to court personnel, lawyers and creditors, and to have your personal finances placed under court control.

- When you walk out of bankruptcy court after signing the final papers, you will still have shoes on. Most states allow you to protect a certain amount of home equity. In some states (*Florida, Iowa, Kansas, Minnesota and Oklahoma*) you may even be able to keep your home, no matter what it's worth. Most states will allow you to keep home furnishings, clothing, household goods, pensions and retirement accounts, so don't sell these off or empty out these accounts to pay off your debts unless you are certain you will never file for bankruptcy.

- Don't expect to be allowed to keep expensive luxury items like jewelry, boats, multiple cars or other big-ticket items.

While there are significant negatives to declaring bankruptcy, there are some benefits, even beyond having a chance to start over:

- Certain kinds of debts can be wiped away completely, or discharged. Typically, these are:
    - —Credit card debts
    - —Auto loans
    - —Rent payments
    - —Medical bills
    - —Utility bills

- By the same token, certain kinds of debt cannot be discharged. These are:

    —Child support

    —Alimony

    —Taxes *(both state and federal)*

    —Court-ordered fines or damages

A final note about bankruptcy: With your slate wiped clean of the worst of your debts, you are getting a do-over. This means you can breathe easily for the first time in a long while. You can answer the phone again and stop cringing whenever you open your mail. This does not mean that you can go right out and spend like there's no tomorrow. One bankruptcy experience should be enough for anyone. Get credit counseling and resolve to learn from your past mistakes. Now is the time to start working toward a reasonable financial future and retirement.

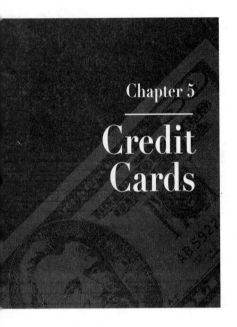

Chapter 5

Credit Cards

The credit card is a recent invention. Store credit cards began being issued in your grandparents' days, but the mega-card, accepted all over the place, was a product of the 1960s. Today, even high school students carry multiple credit cards for gas and personal purchases. People who swore they'd never use credit cards now find they have several. It seems as if you can't even open a bank account these days without the bank's card being a part of the package. Unless you have an incredibly horrible credit history, your daily mail is filled with credit card solicitations, each one offering a sweeter deal than the last, at least for an "introductory period."

However, without a credit card, it's difficult to take care of many basic transactions, like as making airline or other travel reservations, or making Internet purchases. Credit cards also make life easier in other ways – by offering a quick and safer way to pay for large purchases, for instance. Few of us want to walk around with hundreds of dollars in our wallets or purses. Although a credit card can be stolen, it's a lot easier to minimize card losses than it is to recover a wad of cash.

Proper use of a credit card will help you develop a solid, respectable credit record. Any lender will look at your payment records to see if you are reliable and trustworthy as far as paying off your debts on time, and in the right amounts.

But credit cards can be dangerous as well, particularly when you are young and just starting out. Even the most sensible people can get caught up in a spending spree and lose track of their total debt. In fact, in a recent survey that evaluated credit card use among college students, it was determined that:

- More than 80 percent of all college undergraduates have a credit card. 40 percent of these students reported having three or more credit cards.
- The average college student has a credit card debt of more than $3,000 when they graduate.

Before you become another credit card debt statistic, learn how to handle a credit card wisely.

The Value Of Credit Cards

Credit cards provide a variety of benefits. Following are a few of the primary benefits credit cards can provide.

Convenience & Emergency Use
Credit cards allow you to pay for things when you don't have cash on hand and personal checks can't be used. For example, if your car breaks down or you need to make an emergency trip home, a credit card would come in handy. It also provides a thorough record of your transactions.

Establishing Credit
Credit cards allow you to establish a record of your ability to effectively manage your finances. In addition, having a good credit history will be important when you are ready to apply for a loan, rent an apartment and, in some cases, apply for a job.

Security
Carrying large amounts of cash can be risky and dangerous. Credit cards allow you to make large purchases without having to carry large quantities of cash in your wallet. In addition, while a credit card can be stolen and used, your responsibility for unauthorized purchases is minimal.

Flexibility
Credit cards allow for flexibility in your budget. When properly used, a credit card may give you 45 days or more of free credit. For example, let's say that your credit card has a billing date of the 5th of every month. Payment for that credit card is due by the 15th. Therefore, if you make a purchase on the 6th, that purchase will not show up until the following month and payment will not be due until the 15th of that month. Assuming that you pay off the balance of that purchase on time, you have just been provided use of that credit card company's money for almost 45 days without incurring interest or fees. Note that this only works if you pay the card off completely each month. If you carry a monthly balance, you begin to accrue finance charges from the time of purchase.

Insurance Protection

Many credit cards provide some type of insurance coverage or protection on purchases made with the card. For example, say you bought an item online and it wasn't delivered, but your credit card was charged. If the vendor you purchased the item from will not agree to refund your money, you can dispute the charge with your credit card company. In most cases the credit card company will refund your money while they investigate the situation. Other forms of insurance coverage may include free collision coverage on rental cars and protection from charges made to your credit card if it is stolen.

The details and specifics of insurance coverage and your rights and responsibilities in a dispute vary from credit card company to credit card company. Therefore, contact credit card companies you are considering and ask them to provide details and examples of how the insurance coverage and protections can benefit you.

Travel Reservations

Most airlines, hotels and other travel-related industries now require a credit card number to hold a reservation. While you can use cash, you are required to go to the ticketing office to do so, and that can mean an expensive trip downtown or a long trip to an airport.

Overseas Travel

It is very hard to travel today without a major credit card. You will find that most business establishments in foreign countries cheerfully accept your credit card. Dealing with foreign currency can be cumbersome and confusing, while a credit card company automatically does the monetary conversion, and gives you the prevailing rate. In case of an overseas emergency, a credit card is a must – it speaks all languages.

Consolidate Debt

Many credit cards invite you to apply for their services, and offer as an enticement the chance for you to consolidate your debt to one card. Check the rates and determine how long these offers are valid. It might make sense to take advantage of such an offer if the math looks good. There is also the convenience of paying one debt instead of a number of smaller ones.

Credit Cards—What You Need To Know And Do

Credit cards offer a number of benefits for judicious users. However, due to easy access to credit and a lack of budgeting skills, some credit card users can find themselves extended beyond their means. To avoid using more credit than you can afford to, follow these tips:

Have Only One Credit Card

Very few people need multiple credit cards. As a college graduate, one credit card should be sufficient for your needs. Find a single credit card that offers the advantages you need and cancel any other cards you may have.

Stop Applying for Credit Cards

Credit card companies will create all kinds of gimmicks to get you to apply for their credit cards, including offering free T-shirts, stuffed animals, travel vouchers, etc. Even if you don't intend to use the credit card you are applying for, don't apply for it. Every time you apply for a credit card it is recorded in your credit history. Applying for too many cards can reflect negatively on your credit rating. This can cause serious problems when you are trying to apply for some form of credit your really need at a later time, like for a car or home.

Avoid Reward Credit Cards

Some credit card companies offer credit cards that can be used to earn free stuff, like free airline travel. These types of credit cards usually charge an annual fee for their usage, with the fees ranging from $50 to $100. Although earning free airline travel or other items for simply charging normal expenses to your credit card may seem like a great deal, the fees often outweigh the benefits.

Before applying for one of these credit cards, be sure to evaluate your potential use of the card. In almost all cases, you are better off saving the annual fee and applying the savings toward the item the credit card company is offering. In addition, the airline travel you earn from a credit card company usually comes with a number of stipulations that limit when you can travel.

Request a Lower Credit Limit

Credit card companies have a habit of giving you a higher line of credit than you really need. If you find that it's difficult to manage the amount you charge to your credit card and you are unwilling to part with your card, contact your credit card company and request that they lower your available credit to a limit you know you can pay off every month. It's hard to imagine a recent graduate who would need a credit limit of $10,000.

Use Only When Necessary

Credit cards are convenient to use – sometimes too convenient. If you have the ability to pay for an item or service with cash or a check, do so. Charging items to your credit card can give you a false sense of your financial situation, particularly if you do not keep track of your charges.

Keep a Journal

One of the problems with credit cards is that you often lose track of your credit card balance until the statement arrives each month. Be sure to keep track of your credit card purchases, just as you keep track of the checks you write with a check register. By keeping a journal of your credit card purchases throughout the month, you will be aware of the exact outstanding balance on your card. Many credit card companies now offer their customers the ability to manage their accounts online. If this service is offered, use it regularly to monitor your purchases.

Pay More Than the Minimum Due

If you experience a situation where you are unable to pay off the entire balance due when your credit card bill comes, always pay off as much as you possibly can. Interest charges can accumulate quickly. Also, if you have the ability to pay off the balance due prior to the arrival of the next bill, consider sending in your payment early. Interest charges are commonly calculated on a daily basis. Therefore, the sooner you pay off your balance, the fewer interest charges you will accumulate.

Avoid Late Fees

Late fees are expensive and unnecessary. In addition, they can wreak havoc on your credit report. Always pay your bill on time, even if it is only the minimum payment. If you get into a situation where you cannot pay your bill on time, contact your credit card company. They may be able to lower the minimum payment amount, or possibly change the due date so that your bill can be paid at a more convenient time during the month.

Get a Better Deal

On average, it costs credit card companies anywhere from $50 to $150 in marketing costs to acquire a new customer. Therefore, when they get a customer they want to keep that customer. This can work to your advantage. For example, if you want a lower interest rate, the annual fee waived, or a late payment fee voided, simply call your credit card company and ask. The credit card company representative is trained to resist, but if you stick to your guns, chances are you will prevail. If all else fails, threaten to cancel your credit card or transfer your balance to a competing credit card. You will be surprised what a credit card company is willing to do in order to keep you as a customer.

Avoid First-Time Use Discount Promotions

Beware of a ploy used by department and larger specialty and discount stores: the one-time 10 percent off of your first purchase when you open an account with that store. Although this sounds like a good deal, unless your savings are significant, or you have the ability to pay off the balance ASAP, don't do it. In addition, the interest rates on these cards are usually high—up to 15 percent.

Read Everything!

Finally, although it is painfully boring, it is important that you read everything that comes in the mail or is stuffed into the bill from your credit card company. They will send policy changes and new fee schedules, and make it look so dreary you just can't wait to toss it, but beware of the fine print. For example, you may have been lucky enough to obtain a "no annual fee" card, but if you miss the notice that says they will start charging you a fee unless you send back confirmation that you don't want to be charged the fee, you will be stuck with the new fee.

The Cost of Credit Cards

Oftentimes credit card users fail to realize the true cost of their credit card debt. The following example and chart will provide you with a better understanding of what credit card debt can costs you.

Jack just landed his first job out of college and rented his first apartment. In his mail one day was an offer for a free T-shirt. All he had to do was complete a simple application for a credit card. He really wanted the T-shirt, so he applied for the card. A couple of weeks later his new credit card arrived. Jack was ecstatic about receiving his new credit card and wanted to try it out, so he went shopping. The next month his first credit card bill arrived. He was surprised to see that he had accumulated $2,000 in charges. However, when he saw that he only needed to pay a minimum of $60, or 3 percent of the balance, he was relieved. He sent the $60 payment and decided to stop using the credit card until he paid off the balance. Unfortunately, Jack didn't realize that his new credit card had an interest rate of 18 percent. How long will it take Jack to pay off his balance? How much will Jack end up paying before his new credit card balance is fully paid?

Number of Months to Pay-Off a
Credit Card Balance

Payment as a % of Initial Debt	Annual Interest Rate					
	8%	10%	12%	14%	16%	18%
2%	61	65	70	75	83	93
3%	38	39	41	42	44	47
4%	27	28	29	30	31	32
5%	21	22	22	23	23	24
10%	10	10	11	11	11	11
15%	7	7	7	7	7	7
20%	5	5	5	5	5	5
25%	4	4	4	4	4	4

According to this chart, it will take Jack 47 months to pay off his balance at a cost of $820 in interest charges.

What Is Worse – Annual Fees Or Interest Rates?

So what is better, a credit card with an annual fee and a lower interest rate, or a credit card with no annual fee and a higher interest rate? It depends. Certainly, if you pay off the entire balance due each month, a credit card with no annual fee is the best option, since the higher interest rate is not relevant. However, the decision becomes a bit more difficult if you carry a credit card balance month to month. Consider the following example.

Let's say you are deciding between two different credit cards. The first card has a $25 annual fee and a 13 percent interest rate. The second card has no annual fee and a 15 percent interest rate.

Average Monthly Balance	No Annual Fee 15 Percent Interest	$25 Annual Fee 13 Percent Interest
$1,000	$130	$150
$5,000	$650	$750
$10,000	$1,300	$1,500

If your average monthly balance is $5,000, the no-fee card would cost you an extra $100 a year in interest. Thus, choosing the fee-based credit card is the better deal. But notice how this will vary according to your balance and interest rate. Therefore, take the time to do some comparison-shopping for credit cards. With all the cards available, you ought to be able to find one that is right for you.

Comparing Credit Cards

Credit cards have gotten a lot more complicated over the last decade or so. Gone is the simple card where you paid a small fee and charged your purchases, and that was that. Competition being what it is today, you can get airline miles, free groceries, discounts on goods or services, or just plain old cash rebates.

Shopping for a credit card that has the advantages you need, at the lowest cost and best interest rate, can be confusing, but also quite rewarding. Using the following credit card comparison chart makes the process easy. As you evaluate different credit cards, plug in the information into this chart and see how they compare. You may be surprised at what you find.

When filling out the following chart, if you are unable to find certain information about a credit card, or if the information is confusing, contact the credit card company and ask them to provide you with the information you need.

Credit Card Comparison Chart

Feature	Example Card A	Example Card B	Your Card
Interest Rate	14.50%	17.50%	
Index Rate	Prime	Prime	
Cash Advance Charges	21%	21%	
Over-the-Limit Charges	21%	21%	
Annual Fee	$35	$30	

Credit Card Fraud

Being a victim of credit card fraud is a scary, time-consuming and costly experience. In fact, victims of credit card fraud spend an average of 175 hours and up to $800 just to clear their names. Following are some tips on how you can protect yourself from credit card fraud:

- Always keep your credit card statements and receipts in a safe, accessible location.

- If you can access your account online, check it at least once a week for unauthorized charges.

- Actually review the paper copy of your credit card statement instead of glancing over it. Be on the lookout for unauthorized charges.

- Call your credit card company if your monthly statement is late.

- Drop off your credit card payment into a secure post office box, not your own mailbox. Thieves frequently steal credit card information from mailboxes.

- Pay your bill online if you have a secure computer and Internet access.

- Never give your credit card number over the phone to strangers. The simple rule is that if the person called you—as opposed to you calling them—assume the worst, and do not give out your number. Crooks make a point of sounding very nice.

- Do not use your credit card on Internet sites you don't trust.

- When you throw away documents with your credit card number on them, be sure to tear them up sufficiently – or, better yet, use a paper shredder.

- Keep the telephone number of your credit card company in a location other than your wallet so if your credit card is stolen with your wallet, you can contact the credit card company immediately.

For more information on protecting yourself from credit card fraud and identity theft, review the Identity Theft chapter.

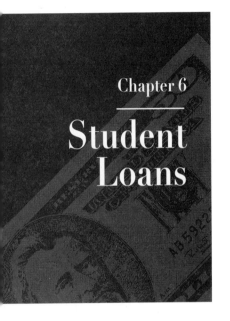

Chapter 6

Student Loans

As you read in the Debt Management chapter, there is good debt and there is bad debt. Student loans are "good" debt because they represent an investment in your future, they come in a variety of types, and offer flexibility in both how you can borrow and repay. But, like any debt, a student loan must be repaid or you – and your credit rating – will suffer. So it's good to know what's involved in a loan, how they work, and what your options are.

What Type of Loan(s) Do You Have?

As you may remember when you applied for your loan, there are a variety of loan types. Here are of the most common types:

- Federal Stafford Loans *(subsidized and unsubsidized)*
- Signature Student Loans
- Perkins Loans
- FFELP (Federal Family Education Loan Program) Loans

Since each type of loan has its own requirements, it's a good idea to review what type of loan or loans you have and what each one involves. If you don't know what loans you have, there are resources on the Web to help. Check out the loan locator service at the National Student Clearinghouse site www.studentclearinghouse.org. You should be able to find a complete list of your outstanding loans.

Since most student loans are somehow related to Sallie Mae *(the federal government's student loan marketing association)* you can also check with them at www.salliemae.com. In addition to helping you identify what type of loan you have, there's a lot of very useful information on the site.

Understanding Your Loan(s)

So, you've found your loan, or loans. Now what? There are two major areas to explore: Repayment Options and Interest Rates. Both will impact your loan and your lifestyle while you're repaying your loan.

Repayment Options

Repayment Options are just what they sound like – different choices on how to make payments on your loan. If you have a subsidized loan *(where the government pays the interest on the loan while you are in school)*, you've got the best deal going. With an unsubsidized loan, you still don't make payments while you're in school, but the interest accumulates unpaid, meaning you'll pay more after you graduate. Sallie Mae has a calculator to help you figure out how much more you have to pay.

Here's some good news: you can choose a repayment plan that fits your income. Here are some of the standard plans:

- **Flex Repay** – "Interest only" payments for up to four years. Since you pay no principle, just interest on the loan, this is particularly good if your income is low, or fluctuates.

- **Income-Based Repayment** – Payments are calculated as a percentage of your income.

- **Extended Repayment** – Lenders, including Sallie Mae, may allow you up to 25 years to repay your loan.

- **Graduated Plan** – Payments grow as your income does, and get larger as you earn more.

- **Direct Repay** – An automatic payment is drawn from your checking account each month. Sallie Mae currently reduces your interest rate by one-quarter percent if you pick this option. Depending on how large your loan is, that seemingly small quarter-of-a-percent could add up to a tidy savings.

- **Net Repay** – An online payment option from Sallie Mae, this works through your bank or payment service. Not only is this an easy way to repay, it also qualifies for that one-quarter percent reduction in your interest rate.

Interest Rates

Another very important piece of information to have is the interest rate on each of your loans. Even the government doesn't hand out money for free. For instance:

- Stafford Loans charge a lower rate while you're in school, and a somewhat higher when you begin to repay the loan. The interest rate is subject to change each year, but has a cap of 8.25 percent.
- Perkins Loans have a set interest rate, and you don't have to make interest payments while you're in school.
- Bank loans vary, so you should check with your lender to be sure you understand how interest is applied to your loan.

Loan Consolidation

If you have more than one student loan, you may want to consider consolidating them into a single loan with a single monthly payment. Here are some of the advantages:

- Lower interest rates may be available, depending on the program.
- Simplified bill paying and record keeping.
- A longer repayment period.
- A guaranteed interest rate, instead of a variable rate.
- Reduced monthly payments.

Because some loan programs reduce your interest rate if you make on-time payments, be sure to consider this before consolidating under a fixed interest rate loan. But if a fixed rate will make your life simpler, Sallie Mae offers a consolidation program called Smart Loan that offers a fixed, low interest rate for the life of the loan.

Sallie Mae also offers a loan consolidation calculator on their Web site. Check it out.

Another handy web site is www.manageyourloans.com. You'll notice that it's managed by Sallie Mae – probably the best source of information on student loans.

Remember, though, that the government lets you consolidate your loans only once, so be sure it's the right time to take this step. Solicitations for loan consolidation from companies other than your loan holder may look attractive, but are almost always a bad deal. Talk to your lender first.

Deferment And Forbearance

What happens if you run into financial trouble? You still have to repay your loan, but there are options:

Deferment

Allows you relief, if you qualify. If you have a Stafford Loan, the government will make the interest payments for you. If not, you make the interest payments, but pay nothing on the principle. You can qualify for deferment for these reasons:

- Unemployment
- Enrollment in school
- Graduate fellowship
- Financial hardship
- Enrollment in a rehabilitation program because of a disability

Forbearance

Allows temporary reduction or postponement of principle payments. Forbearance programs are managed by your lender, so you must talk to them. In a forbearance period, interest continues to accrue, and if you opt not to pay it, it's added to the loan balance. Certain programs, like a medical internship, service in AmeriCorps or active-duty military service automatically qualify you for forbearance.

Keep in mind that your student loan payment history is part of your credit report, and bad credit can have far-reaching consequences.

Forgiveness Of Loans

Sometimes student loans will be "forgiven," – meaning you are not required to repay them. This happens only under special circumstances:

- Teaching full-time in a low-income school for five years. Your lender can help you apply for this program.
- Spending two years as a child care provider serving a low-income community. Both Sallie Mae and the Department of Education have more information on this option.
- Becoming a registered nurse who serves an area with a nursing shortage. More information can be found at the Department of Health and Human Services Web site.

Discounts

There are ways to save money as you repay your student loan. As mentioned under the Repayment Options section, both Direct Repay and NetPay will reduce your interest rates by one-quarter-of-a percentage point. These programs are managed by Sallie Mae. Other ways to save include:

- **On-Time Payments** – Some lenders, including Sallie Mae, will reduce interest rates or offer credits if you maintain a record of paying on time.

- **Early Repayment** – Increasing your monthly payment will reduce the amount of principle you owe, and thus reduce the total amount of interest you'll have to pay over the life of the loan.

Check with your lender to see if other discounts are available.

Tax Benefits

If you're earning money, you're paying taxes. Your student loan interest payments may reduce your tax burden. While there are many criteria that must be met, a portion of your annual interest may be deductible. Those criteria, like so much associated with loans, are complicated:

- The loan must have been used for tuition, fees, room and board, supplies and other related items.

- Certain income limits must be met. Because limits change from year to year, you should check the IRS Web site www.irs.gov for current information to determine if you qualify.

- Your lender will provide a Form 1098-E if your interest payments exceed $600 in any one year.

- You must use Form 1040 or Form 1040A when filing your taxes.

Defaulting On Your Student Loan

The federal government used to be a lot less diligent about going after people who don't make regular payments on student loans. But not any more. If your payments are nine months late, you're in default. Your lender will then file a claim and your loan will be assigned to a collection agency. Credit bureaus also are notified. This is not a good situation.

A number of very unpleasant consequences follow default:

- Federal income tax refunds can be withheld and applied to the loan.

- Wages can be garnished.

- You could be liable for collection costs – up to 40 percent of the loan!

- Professional certificates and licenses *(law, medical, accounting)* can be revoked.

- You could lose eligibility for further financial aid.

- You could lose eligibility for other federal loan programs like Federal Housing Administration and Veterans Affair mortgage loans.

- You may be denied other kinds of credit – from credit cards to car loans.
- The government can, and will, sue you and take your assets *(car, savings, etc.)*.
- Your credit rating will suffer.

If you find yourself in a tight spot with your repayment program, you do have options:

- Change your repayment plan.
- Consolidate your loans.
- Apply for forbearance or deferment.

Whatever path you choose, talk to your lender as soon as you know you're going to have trouble with your repayment schedule. The earlier you do this, the better.

If your loan is in default, the entire loan, plus unpaid interest, is due and must be paid at once. If you wind up in default, you still have several choices:

- Pay off the loan in its entirety.
- Establish a new monthly payment schedule with the collector.
- Consolidate the loan with any other bills you may have. This new loan replaces the old, defaulted loan.

The federal government does offer a rehabilitation program for people with student loans. You must make 12 on-time payments in a row and then apply for rehabilitation. Once you've rehabilitated your loan, you have nine years in which to repay it. But this is a one-time deal – you can only rehabilitate a student loan once.

Keep in mind that, by law, you are not required to pay more than you can reasonably afford on your student loan – talk to your lender early, and ask about a reasonable and affordable repayment plan. This is a far better option than default.

Bankruptcy And Student Loans

Bankruptcy is an option for people who have no other way out, but be aware that student loans are treated differently in bankruptcy. Basically, student loans will not be dismissed in a bankruptcy filing unless paying back the student loan would cause extreme and undue hardship. And even then, the court's definitions of hardship are very tough to meet. Generally speaking, if you qualify for the bankruptcy court's definition of hardship, you also qualify to have your loan cancelled. Cancellation is a better choice.

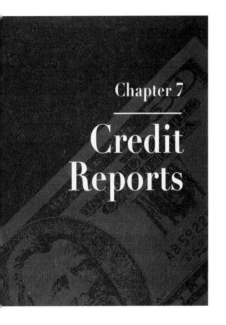

Chapter 7

Credit Reports

Few people realize that when you sign up for a new credit card, apply for a student loan, apply to rent an apartment, or even accept a new job, you may be giving the bank, the landlord, or the hiring company, permission to review your credit report. Do you know what your credit report could tell them? You should. A credit report can help or hurt you in a lot of ways. Understanding what it's comprised of and how information is recorded in your report makes you a savvier consumer.

Every time you apply for, or accept, a loan or other form of credit, this information is added to your credit report. More importantly, this report records how you use your credit and how much of it you have available. It also keeps track of your ability to repay that credit. In a way, it's your credit report card.

So why is this information important to you now? Well, there are many reasons. Most importantly, your credit report represents your ability to handle financial responsibilities. The more responsible you are, the easier it will be for you to obtain financial assistance later in life.

Credit Report & Credit Score – What Are They?

Your entire financial credit history is compiled by one of several credit bureaus and then organized into the following formats.

Credit Report
This report contains a detailed history of all your borrowing habits for the past seven to ten years.

Credit Score
A credit score is a shorthand way for a lender to tell if you're a good credit risk or a bad one. The information from your credit report is calculated to

determine the financial risk you present to various lending agents (*landlord, employer, credit card company, bank, etc.*).

Lenders rarely spend much time evaluating the specific details of your credit report. What they are interested in is how these details form your overall credit score. People with the highest scores get the most favorable interest rates and can save a lot of money. If your score is very low, you may not qualify for any credit at all. Your credit score is made up of five factors:

- **Your ability to make payments on time** – Paying on time is good; missing payments consistently will lower your score.

- **The amount of credit you owe** – The total amount you owe on your credit cards, car loans, mortgages, etc.

- **The length of your credit history** – The longer you've had credit, the higher your score. This is one of those "not fair" things, especially if you're just starting to build your credit history.

- **The type of credit you owe** – A mixture of revolving credit (*e.g., credit cards*) and installment credit (*e.g., mortgages*) is statistically a better risk.

- **The number of requests for new credit** – How many credit applications you've made.

While lenders are interested in your credit score, you should also be concerned about the specific details of your credit report and what steps you need to take to raise your overall credit score. Why? Because a lousy credit score means you'll pay higher interest rates on credit you're able to get. In extreme circumstances, a bad credit score means no credit at all.

What Does A Credit Report Say About You?

Credit reports are made up of five basic parts:

- **Personal Information** – your name, telephone number, current and previous addresses, Social Security number, date of birth, as well as a list of your current and previous employers.

- **Credit History** – including any late payments to banks, credit card companies, retailers and other lenders. This information remains on your credit report for seven years.

- **Public Records** – any debts owed to a creditor or tax agency that you have failed to pay. In addition, any filings of personal bankruptcy or court judgments against you are included. These remain on your credit report for seven years, except bankruptcies, which stick around for ten years.

- **Inquiries** – when you seek to obtain credit or authorize someone to access your credit report, these actions are recorded. The length of time these items remain on your credit report varies by credit bureau.
- **Current Credit** – amounts owed, amounts available, and payment amounts on installment loans.

When you evaluate the details of your credit report, consider the answers to these questions: How good are you at managing credit? How reliable are you at making payments on time? Do you take your obligations seriously? The answers can mean the difference between getting a loan (*or a credit card or a job*) or not.

Who Has The Right To See Your Credit Report?

Any person or organization permitted to see the information contained in your credit report can see it. This can include lenders, your employer, and even your landlord. There are two types of credit inquiries that can be made to your credit report:

Hard Inquiries
A hard inquiry happens when you authorize someone to access your credit report. This includes applying for credit cards or authorizing your employer or landlord to access your credit report. These inquiries are recorded on your report. Lenders and other creditors worry when they see a large number of hard inquiries because it suggests either a lack of responsibility or an effort to borrow beyond your means.

Soft Inquiries
A soft inquiry is not a bona fide request for credit. For example, if you ask for a copy of your credit report (*which is your right under the law*), this would be a soft inquiry. Soft inquiries are not recorded as part of your credit report. Soft inquiries also happen when a company gathers potential marketing information about you based on your credit report – for instance, those unsolicited offers for credit cards you get in the mail. If you don't want these kinds of offers, the Fair Credit Reporting Act says you can contact the major credit bureaus and ask them to stop sending you card solicitations and other offers. To learn more about this program, call 888-5-OPT-OUT/(567-8688).

When Should You Get A Copy Of Your Credit Report?

If you're serious about managing your credit, you should review your credit report on an annual basis. Be sure to get reports from each of the three major reporting companies. An annual review will let you take care of problems before they impact your creditworthiness. It will also help protect you from credit reporting errors and allow you to spot identity theft.

Other times you may want to obtain a copy of your credit report:

- Prior to applying for a large loan, like a car or home loan.
- Prior to applying for a job.
- After major life changes, like a marriage or divorce.
- After being denied credit when a credit report was used in making the decision.

When you receive a copy of your credit report, don't assume that the information from one credit bureau is the same as the information from other credit bureaus. Each bureau operates separately. Get a copy from all the major credit bureaus, compare the information, and be prepared to fix any errors you find.

How Do You Get A Copy Of Your Credit Report?

A recent amendment to the federal Fair Credit Reporting Act requires each of the nationwide consumer reporting companies *(Equifax, Experian, and TransUnion)* to provide you with a free copy of your credit report, at your request, once every 12 months.

Because this is a new program, it is being introduced in phases. However, everyone will have access to free credit reports by September 1, 2005. To learn more about the free credit report program, visit the Federal Trade Commission's Web site at www.ftc.gov.

If you are not currently eligible for a free credit report and you need one, by all means invest in purchasing one. The fee is minimal – less than $10 – and taking action now may save you from a lot of problems in the future.

You can obtain a free copy of your credit report from the following major credit bureaus:

Equifax	Experian	TransUnion
800-685-1111	888-397-3742	800-888-4213
www.equifax.com	www.experian.com	www.transunion.com

How Do You Fix Mistakes In Your Credit Report?

Credit bureaus are required to investigate any claim of errors in, or omissions from, your credit report within 30 days. But you have to let them know you suspect an error. Once a claim is made, the credit bureau contacts the creditor in question and investigates the claim. If an error exists, the creditor must correct it and notify all major credit bureaus of the error. In addition, the credit bureau that originally reported the error must send you a free copy of your revised credit report to show that the error has been corrected.

If your credit report contains an error or omission:

- **Document your claim** – Write a letter to the credit bureau explaining your dispute, send any information that substantiates your claim, and request that the error be corrected.

- **Inform the creditor** – Although it is the responsibility of the credit bureau to contact the creditor in question, it's always a good idea to inform the creditor of your dispute as well. This way you can be assured the creditor receives all the information you provided to the credit bureau.

- **Send copies** – Never send original documents. In some cases, that document may be the only proof you have to substantiate your claim.

- **Keep records** – Document all correspondence you receive from the credit bureau and creditor and document all phone conversations. Include dates, times, and the names of the people involved.

- **Track information** – Whenever you send materials via the post office or other carrier, or by fax, e-mail or any other means, always keep track of when the information was sent and when it was received.

If your claim is denied and you don't agree with the outcome, you do have a few other options available.

- Write a short statement of 100 words or less and have the credit agency include it in your credit report. This information will then be sent to whoever requests a copy of your credit report. At your request, the credit bureau must send a copy of the updated version of your credit report, free of charge, to anyone who has recently received the previous version.

- Contact the U.S. Federal Trade Commission's consumer help line at 877-FTC-HELP or visit www.ftc.gov. Inform the representative of your situation and request their assistance.

What If You're Denied Credit?

If your application for credit is denied, federal law states that the lender must provide you an explanation for the rejection. If the denial was based on your credit report, the lender must provide you the name and address of the credit agency that provided the report. When you are denied credit, all credit bureaus are required by law to send you a free copy of your credit report (*if you request it*) within 30 days.

What If You Have Bad Credit?

If you've been paying attention and have followed our tips and suggestions in this book, you shouldn't have this problem. However, if you're overextended or overwhelmed by the amount of debt you owe, take action now to correct your mistakes. A number of credit counseling services are available to help you.

Credit counseling helps consumers improve their debt-management habits and take the appropriate steps toward improving their credit. These services are not free, but are excellent investments that will help you get your financial life in order. Should you choose to invest in one of these services, be sure to do the following:

- **Ask about fees** – High charges or vague answers are a sure sign you should look elsewhere. Do yourself a favor and shop around for the best rate you can find.

- **Ask if they are accessible** – Check out their hours or whether you can deal with them online or on the phone. Your life is already too complicated to have to rearrange your schedule to visit these people.

- **Ask if their employees are paid on commission** – These people, like used-car salesmen, are more interested in their own income than your debt problems.

- **Ask if they offer educational courses on debt management** – The more you can learn about managing/controlling your debt the better.

- **Avoid "quick-fix" firms** – Beware of the slick, late-night television ads or Internet pop-ups that promise they can fix any credit problem. There is no such thing as a "quick-fix."

- **Contact the Better Business Bureau** – Complaints to the Better Business Bureau about irresponsible credit counseling firms are on the rise. Check to see if the agency you are considering is accredited by the Council on Accreditation or other accreditation services.

Additional information about credit counseling services can be found in the Debt Management chapter.

Chapter 8

Identity Theft

I dentity theft is a serious problem. In fact, it is estimated that at least 10 million people are victims of identity theft each year – costing its victims $5 billion, and businesses more than $50 billion. And these numbers continue to rise. Will you be the next victim? It depends. Have you recently written a check, made a purchase over the Internet, thrown away a credit card solicitation? If so, your identity has the potential to be compromised.

How Does Identity Theft Occur?

The Federal Trade Commission says that 43 percent of complaints filed with the agency in 2002 were reports of identity theft. And the number continues to grow because identity theft has become so simple – primarily because of the accessibility of personal information. Thanks, in part, to the Internet.

While there are a lot of electronic methods to obtain information, identity thieves frequently rely on simpler methods, like stealing your purse or wallet, taking mail from your mailbox, or fishing documents out of your trash. It's easier than you may think.

Another, more recent, form of identity theft occurs by "phishing" or "spoofing." This occurs when a thief sends an e-mail that looks legitimate – that perhaps, seems to be from your bank – and requests account information or passwords to address some problem, usually a compromised account. If you respond by clicking on the handy link, you'll be routed to a Web site that looks real, but isn't. Think about it: Your bank already has your account numbers. Only a thief would ask for them by e-mail.

What Thieves Do With Your Information

Identity thieves are good at what they do. As soon as they steal your information, they can run up thousands of dollars of debt in a matter of minutes. Pre-approved credit offers taken from your mail or trash can be activated. After they complete a "change of address" form, you'll never lay eyes on the new card or the bill. Often an identity thief will call your creditor to change the mailing address for your credit card. You won't know anything's wrong until months later, when the creditor calls you about a huge, past-due bill. With your Social Security number, anyone can open a bank account in your name, deposit a minimum amount and then write dozens of bad checks. And guess who the bank will call when they process all of those checks and there aren't sufficient funds in the account to pay them?

How Can You Minimize Your Risk?

There are a number of things you can do to prevent yourself from becoming a victim of identity theft:

- **Purchase a shredder** – Inexpensive shredders are available at every office supply store. Shred all pieces of mail (*receipts or papers, including deposit slips, bills, statements and voided checks*) that have account numbers on them, including those pre-approved credit card offers.

- **Be aware of your billing cycles** – If a bill does not arrive when it should, call the company and track it down. A diverted bill could be a sign of a compromised account.

- **Never provide personal information** – Unless you have initiated the contact, never give out personal information. No legitimate bank, credit card company, online shopping or auction site, etc., will ask you for this information.

- **Mail bills from a post office** – Instead of mailing your bills from your personal mailbox, where they easily can be stolen, take them to the post office. For maximum security, rent a post office box and have everything delivered there.

- **Do not give out your Social Security Number (SSN)** – Never give out your SSN unless you absolutely must. If your state's Department of Motor Vehicles (DMV) has this option, use a DMV-generated ID number on your driver's license instead of your SSN.

- **Do not allow your SSN to be printed on your checks.**

- **Do not carry your Social Security card in your wallet.** Store your Social Security card and other important papers – like your passport – in a secure location, preferably a bank box or secure lockbox.

- **Remove your information from marketing databases** – This can be done by e-mailing or writing to the following organizations:

> **Direct Marketing Association**
> Telephone Preference Service
> P.O. Box 1559
> Carmel, NY 10512
> www.the-dma.org

> **Direct Mail Marketing Association**
> Mail Preference Service
> P.O. Box 643
> Carmel, NY 10512
> www.dma.consumers.org

- **Check your credit report** - Order a copy of your credit report at least once a year through all three of the major credit reporting agencies. Review your report for any errors or omissions and take steps to correct any errors you find as soon as possible. Additional information on credit reports can be found in the Credit Report chapter.

Protecting Yourself On The Web

So much business is transacted via computers and the Internet that it has become a playground for identity theft. Here are some basic steps to protect your identity while you're on the Web:

- **Protect your passwords** – Never allow your computer to remember your passwords for any Web site. A few simple clicks and an identity thief can have access to your personal information. Also avoid using actual words and important dates or numbers as your password. Instead, scramble letters, throw a few numbers in the middle, use capitals and symbols.

- **Change your passwords frequently** – Change your passwords at least every few months, and never use the same password for multiple Web sites.

- **Invest in virus protection software** – As an additional measure, also avoid opening any "iffy" downloads.

- **Install a firewall** - This is especially important if you have a cable or DSL modem that keeps you connected to the Internet 24 hours a day.

- **Use a secure browser** - This will encrypt or scramble the information you send from your computer.

- **Erase your Web history daily** – Even though you may have logged off from a Web site, your computer keeps a record of that site in its history. All a thief has to do is go to your computer's history file and he or she can go right to the Web site you were viewing earlier. For most computers, erasing your Web history is as easy as clicking "Start," selecting "Settings" and then choosing "Control Panel." Click on "Internet Options," go to "History" and set "Days to Keep" to zero.

- **Never include personal information in an e-mail** – E-mails easily can be intercepted by technologically savvy identity thieves. A good rule of thumb: if you don't want anyone else reading the contents of your e-mail, choose another method of delivering that information.

- **Purchase only from secure Web sites** – When making purchases on the Internet, check for the padlock icon in your browser that indicates you are on a secure site. In addition, read the site's privacy policy. If you are unsure if the site is safe to use, use another vendor.

What To Do If You Are The Victim Of Identity Theft

Quick action is the key to clearing up problems caused by identity theft. As soon as you discover that anything – bank accounts, credit card accounts, anything – has been compromised, take action.

- **File a report with the local police** – Be sure to request a copy of the report. This report will be extremely helpful should a creditor or other financial organization require proof that your identity has been compromised.

- **Contact the fraud sections of the three major credit reporting companies** – Ask them to place a "fraud alert" in your file.

- **Contact the fraud unit of your credit card company** – If your credit account has been compromised or a credit account has been opened in your name, close the account immediately. Make a note of who you speak to, the date, and what was said. Write them a follow-up letter detailing the facts as you know them. Even if your credit account has not been compromised, but one of your other financial accounts has, it may be wise to contact your credit card company and inform them of the situation.

- **Contact the Federal Trade Commission's Identity Theft Hotline** – The FTC will keep a centralized record that can aid law enforcement in catching the thief and assist in clearing your record. You can contact them at 877-438-4338 or at www.consumer.gov.

- **Call the Social Security Administration's Fraud Hotline** – If your SSN has been stolen or compromised, contact the Social Security Administration at 800-269-0271.

- **Contact your bank** – If your bank account information or any other form of your identity has been compromised, contact your bank immediately and inform them of the situation. Inform them of all outstanding checks you have written and request that your current account be closed and a new account opened. Also request that your bank notify check verification companies about the situation.

- **Order credit reports every month for six months, then quarterly** – Review them for any errors or omissions and address any mistakes immediately.

- **Never pay a bill that's not yours** – No matter how much you get hassled, don't pay. Be polite, explain the facts, but be firm. Once you pay, it will be extremely difficult for you to get your money back.

- **Be persistent** – This is your identity you are protecting.

  — Keep careful notes of every conversation. Make note of the date and times these conversations take place.

  — Try to send all correspondence by registered mail, and save the receipts. If you have to use e-mail or regular mail, be sure to save copies.

  — Keep a well-organized file of correspondence, phone numbers, addresses and notes.

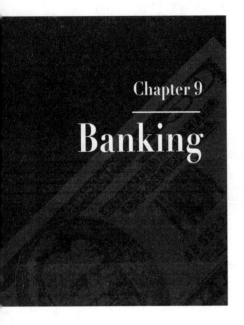

Chapter 9

Banking

How much do you think is fair for you to pay a bank to use their services? Yes, you read that correctly: YOU PAY THE BANK! It just doesn't seem to make sense. Yet, according to the Public Interest Research Group, the average annual fee for a regular checking account at a bank is $228. Where does the $228 come from? It comes from monthly maintenance fees, ATM fees, teller fees, automatic bill payment fees, check-writing fees, overdraft fees – the list goes on and on.

So what is the alternative? Well, you could keep your money in a coffee can and store it in a safe place. Yet that has a price too: The price of lost opportunity and risk – not having the ability to earn interest on your money, and the possibility of losing all your money in the event of theft or fire. The only good alternative is to find a bank that offers you the services you want and need, but doesn't charge you an arm and a leg for those services.

Banks now offer the "convenience" of multiple services. But, as with all complicated financial doings, the devil is in the details. For example, if you do your homework, you can probably get a better deal on a credit card by going directly to the credit card company, which may offer you no annual fee, and cash back on your purchases to boot. So, too, can you possibly get a better car loan through a dealership anxious to move cars off their lot. Bank savings accounts are notoriously skimpy on interest rates, as well. You may find that you can earn better money using an online money market account, and still have the liquidity and accessibility to your cash that you need.

Another important thing to keep in mind: recent technological developments in online banking have lessened the necessity for the "brick and mortar" bank. Oh, you'll still need an actual bank facility occasionally but, as a rule, most banking activity can now be handled with a few keystrokes and clicks of a mouse.

So, why do you need a bank? Well, there are two things banks can do better than any other financial entity:

- Provide you with an all-purpose checking account.
- Give you 24/7 access to your cash around the world through Automated Teller Machines (ATMs).

The goal of this chapter is to help you choose a bank that offers you the services you want, with the lowest associated costs and highest possible interest rates.

Common Banking Mistakes People Make

- **People tend to keep too much money in their no-interest or low-interest bearing checking accounts** – Instead, you should keep only enough money in the account to pay your bills on time, as well as have adequate spending money. Put the rest in a higher interest-bearing account. If you need to keep your funds liquid and reasonably accessible, investigate money market accounts that provide check-writing privileges. And see the Investing chapter for more information on what to do with your excess money.

- **People think online banking is unsafe and/or hard to use** – Quite the opposite. If you can use a computer, you can figure out how to bank online. And because banks are trying to encourage this "do it yourself" approach, there are rarely fees associated with online banking. As far as cyber-security goes, as long as you practice proper "computer hygiene," such as guarding your password with your life, investing in virus and firewall protection, as well as not checking the "remember me on this computer" box when using your computer, you don't need to be afraid of online banking.

- **People focus on one particular aspect of a bank's offers – like free checking – and fail to examine the entire package the bank offers**. Check out the whole picture. Often free checking promotions are masking higher fees/penalties elsewhere that will quickly erode any savings you get from free checking.

- **People think they need to have a bank that is physically close to their home or office.** While that may have been true in the last millennium, it no longer is. Most people now use ATMs and checks for their banking transactions. In addition, banking services such as certified checks, deposits and money orders can be managed either electronically or by phone. When you do have paper checks to deposit, they can be mailed or deposited at an ATM. If you live or work in an urban area that has banks on every corner, you are likely to be happy with a bank that is located near you. But if banks in your area are few and far between, don't hesitate to explore more distant options for better deals.

- **People think that changing banks is a difficult and painful process** – This process does take some organization and attention to detail, but if another bank is offering a better deal – lower fees and free checking – go for it. These small savings can really add up over time.

Banks—What Are Your Options?

For all intents and purposes, bank and credit unions are very much alike. They offer similar financial services and, in almost all cases, they are insured by the Federal Deposit Insurance Corporation (FDIC) for deposits up to $100,000. Look for signs in the bank or credit union that indicate they are FDIC insured, and if you're not sure they are, ask.

The primary difference between banks and credit unions is who they serve. Banks serve their owners – outside shareholders who are interested in making profits. Banks make these profits by charging customers various service fees and offering low interest rates on deposits. Credit unions, on the other hand, are non-profit, member-owned cooperatives whose members share something in common – like membership in the same labor union, the same employer, or same professional community. Since credit unions are non-profit organizations, they are able to offer their services at a much lower cost, while providing higher interest rates on deposits than banks.

Although choosing a credit union for your banking needs may appear to be the obvious choice because of their small size and streamlined operations, there are some minor downsides to credit unions. These include:

- **Membership requirements** – Federal law regulates credit union membership and, therefore, you need to be part of a particular group to be eligible. Contact local credit unions to determine if you are eligible to join.

- **Limited number of branches** – In some cases, they may only have one actual branch.

- **Smaller network of ATMs** – Credit unions may only own ATMs located at their branch locations. However, to get around this, credit unions may offer their members refunds on a limited number of ATM surcharges each month, or they may partner with other credit unions to allow members free use of the other's ATMs.

- **Insurance on deposits may not apply** – Although in most cases credit unions do provide federally insured protection on deposits up to $100,000, about 3 percent of credit unions do not offer this protection.

- **Cancelled checks are not returned to members** – This is one way credit unions cut costs and pass the savings on to their members. If this is an important feature for you, simply use a checkbook that provides carbon copies of checks you have written. Bear in mind, however, that many banks don't offer this service either, in order to lower their costs.

- **Limited range of services** – Because credit unions are smaller, they are not able to offer the expansive range of services that traditional banks do. However, for most people simply having access to some form of checking account is sufficient for their needs.

For simplicity's sake, the term "bank" will be used throughout this chapter to refer to both banks and credit unions.

Choosing A Bank

As mentioned earlier, your goal is to find a bank that offers you the services you want, with the lowest costs and the highest possible interest rates. You can do this by understanding your banking needs and then doing some comparison-shopping.

Understanding Your Banking Needs
If you currently have a bank account, review your statements from the past six months and complete the following chart. If you do not currently have a bank account, estimate your need for these services.

Banking Use

Services	Month						
	1	2	3	4	5	6	Avg.
# of Checks							
# of ATM Withdrawals							
Fees Paid							
ATM							
Account Maintenance							
Overdraft Fees							
Debit Card Use							

Banking Use Continued

Services	1	2	3	4	5	6	Avg.
Low Balance Penalty							
Returned Check/ NSF							
Other							

Comparison-Shopping

Once you have an idea of your banking needs, you are ready to do some comparison-shopping. Contact several banks in your area and collect information on their services. You may find it helpful to create a chart of the services you are seeking in order to do a side-by-side comparison.

Interest Rates	Online Banking
Number of ATMs	Money Market Accounts
Brokerage Services	Convenient Locations
Insurance Products	Loan Services
Direct Deposit	Online Bill Payment
Certificate of Deposit (CD)	Overdraft Protection
Federal Deposit Insurance	Credit Card Services
Telephone Banking	Personalized Checks

After you have determined what services you need, compare the fees charged for their use. Pay close attention to the fine print and the fees you aren't familiar with. Don't assume that because you haven't incurred these fees in the past that you never will do so. Think about all reasonable eventualities. You don't want to wind up paying a large fee for something you've never given a thought to and didn't know how to avoid. Some common fees to look for and compare:

Overdraft fees	Bounced check fees
Excessive withdrawal fee	Low balance fee
Wire transfer fees	Check printing charges
Out-of-network ATM charges	Electronic bill payment fees
Charges for teller service	Check processing fees
Money order and certified check fees	

Free Checking – Is It Really "Free"?

Banks are infamous for developing gimmicks to get new customers. A number of years ago banks offered free products like a toaster or blender to lure new customers. Now the trend is free checking.

When you hear the term "free checking," the first thing you should ask yourself is "What's the catch?" Remember that banks are businesses looking to make a profit. So how can they make a profit if they are giving away free services? Easy: They simply require high minimum balances, offer low interest rates, and hit you with numerous hidden fees.

Don't be fooled by banking gimmicks. Diligent research, asking lots of questions, and comparison-shopping are the best ways to find the right bank for your needs.

Avoiding Banking Fees

As mentioned before, banks are in the business of making money from the fees they charge you. You can reduce these fees by being an informed customer and understanding how and when fees apply. Following are a few ways to reduce common banking fees.

Use Direct Deposit

If your employer can deposit your paycheck to your bank electronically, take advantage of it. Processing checks is expensive, so most banks will waive certain account maintenance fees if you use direct deposit. A word to the wise: always verify that the deposit has been made on time before you write checks. The last thing you want is to have a bunch of bounced checks to deal with – and do you honestly think your employer will reimburse you for your troubles?

Maintain a Minimum Balance

Most banks require their customers to maintain a minimum balance in their accounts in order to avoid certain account maintenance fees. Be sure you understand how your bank calculates the minimum balance. The two most common methods are minimum daily balance and average daily balance. In a minimum daily balance account, you must maintain the minimum balance every single day. The average daily balance method calculates your daily balances and then divides the total by the number of days in the billing cycle.

To avoid the minimum balance requirements, ask your bank if you can link your various accounts. For example, if you have some money in a savings or money market account in addition to a checking account, the total amount may add up to enough to allow you to avoid incurring the minimum balance fee.

Get Overdraft Protection

Regardless of your financial situation, having overdraft protection is a must. Situations can arise where you may write a check for an amount greater than your balance can cover. For example, you may have written several checks and not realized that your paycheck wasn't deposited on time. To avoid the risk of overdraft fees, set up overdraft protection on your checking account. Overdraft protection most commonly takes the form of an established line of credit or link to your bank credit card. Beware that interest rates can be quite high and you may have to pay a "cash advance fee." If you find you have overdrawn your account, make every effort to pay off the debit as soon as possible. Overdraft protection is far cheaper than bouncing checks, but not if you wind up paying high interest on a "loan" over the long run. And keep in mind that having overdraft protection is not a license for you to run hog-wild writing checks you can't afford.

Keep Your Checkbook Balanced

An unbalanced or sloppy checkbook is likely to wind up costing you money, and not just from your own bank. If you write a check that bounces, you'll be hit with high fees from the merchant you wrote it to, in addition to overdraft charges from your bank. Even if you have overdraft protection, if you don't balance your checkbook every month, you'll be inclined to run over your budget. See the Managing Your Account section, located later in this chapter, to learn how you can better organize and balance your checkbook.

Ask For Discounts and Waived Fees

Banking is a competitive business, and once a bank has you as a customer, they want to keep you. Don't be shy about asking for a better deal or to have a fee waived, particularly if the fee was the result of an honest mistake.

Request Cash When You Use Your Debit Card

Most banks do not charge customers for using debit cards. Therefore, to avoid ATM fees request any extra cash you need when you make a purchase with your debit card.

Limit Transactions and Bank Visits

The more you use the bank's services, the more likely it is that you will incur charges. Be sure you are aware of minimum transaction requirements and fees associated with bank visits. This is where online banking and ATMs come in handy.

Use Your Bank's ATMs

According to a survey of checking accounts conducted by Bankrate.com, the average ATM transaction fee is $1.40. However, as a service to their customers, banks will often waive service fees when you use ATMs your bank maintains or networks with. Contact your bank to find which ATMs you can use without incurring service fees. And remember to make a note in your checkbook of any ATM fees you do incur. These fees can pile up and cause your account to become overdrawn if you don't pay attention.

Don't Order Expensive Checks From Your Bank

Banks, on average, charge between $12 and $17 for a box of 250 checks. There are much cheaper options available. Some banks offer a "no frills" check style for free. It's not pretty, but it serves the purpose – and no one cares or notices how attractive your checks are. If your bank does not offer free check printing, try ordering directly from check-printing companies. These companies often advertise on the Internet, and in the weekend newspaper or mailers. Furthermore, consider changing companies with each order you make. By doing so you will receive first-time customer discounts.

Read the Notices!

You get mailings from your bank—slick, legal-looking flyers full of fine print. You've been tossing that stuff for years without reading them. Don't. Banks can be pretty sly about informing customers about new and increased fees within these notices. Therefore, take the time to review them. If a new or higher fee is announced, do what you must to avoid them. But when the going gets expensive, research your other options. There are plenty of banks out there eager to earn your business.

OnLine Banking

Online banking is a safe, secure and convenient alternative to traditional banking. Everything you need to do is as easy as logging on to the Internet. However, keep in mind that online banking, like any online transaction, is only as safe as you make it. Therefore, protect your password, invest in virus and firewall protection, and never use the "Remember Me" function on your computer.

Banks are more than eager to get their customers to use their online services because it is extremely cost-effective for them. In fact, they will often give their customers incentives for using this service, like waiving normal maintenance fees or raising limits on the number of transactions you can make.

This is one of those win/win situations, because it's cost effective for you, too. Fewer trips to the bank means you have more free time and spend less on gas. In addition, immediate online access to your account allows you to spot and deal with trouble as soon as it happens.

One of the best aspects of online banking, besides direct deposit, is the ability to pay your bills online or through automatic debit. The paper check is becoming more and more obsolete. In fact, most companies who send you a monthly bill now encourage you to pay your bills online using electronic checks or authorized debits. You save time, postage and check costs, and you have an electronic record of your payment. Bear in mind that there is lag time between when you pay the bill electronically and when the vendor receives payment. Therefore, do not wait until the due date to pay the bill. As a general rule, you should pay a bill online at least six business days before the due date. If you are solvent and your life is predictable, you often can arrange for a vendor to automatically deduct your payment each month from your checking account. However, do not do this if you run the risk of overdrafts.

Managing Your Account

Unfortunately, most people make the mistake of balancing their accounts only when their bank statement arrives each month, if they balance their accounts at all. Balancing your account on a regular basis – particularly if you maintain a low account balance – is crucial if you want to avoid costly mistakes. The following steps will help you balance your accounts correctly.

Record All Your Transactions
The increase in use of ATMs, debit cards and online banking has made it more difficult to maintain an accurate record of your transactions. If you have difficulty keeping track of your transactions, you may find the following tips helpful:

- If you use a debit card, keep a register to track your usage.

- Purchase duplicate *(carbon imprint)* checks so you have copies available for reference.

- If you don't have duplicate checks, carry a check register with you so that if you write checks while you're away from home you can keep a clear record of your transactions.

- Write ATM withdrawals and deposits into your account register immediately after the transactions. Pay particular attention to transaction fees and record those, too. You may find it helpful to keep your ATM receipt in your wallet/purse as a reminder to record the transaction later.

- When you deposit funds, note the date the funds were deposited and when they will be available. Also keep a copy of the deposit slip for reference.

- Establish a set time each week – like a Sunday evening – to review your accounts and update any activity you may have forgotten.

- Set up an online account so you can easily check your account balances and recent activity at your convenience.

Store Your Records

Nothing is more frustrating or useless than shoeboxes full of disorganized receipts and paperwork. Buy yourself a file cabinet, filing folders and labels. Sort your paperwork each month and file it. You'll need this stuff at tax time, especially if discrepancies arise.

Balance Your Account Each Month

Balancing a checkbook is not difficult, and it is even easier now that most banks give you the ability to access your account online. Buy an inexpensive calculator. Develop your own system of balancing your checkbook, or use a personal finance program on your computer. Bank statements often offer you a worksheet that you can use. There's no excuse for a sloppy checkbook. Keeping your account balanced will allow you to monitor your spending habits and make adjustments before trouble swamps you.

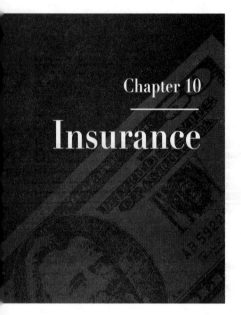

Chapter 10

Insurance

If you're looking for stimulating dinner conversation, insurance probably isn't a suitable topic. If, however, you'd like to protect yourself from financial catastrophe, then there are a few things you need to know about insurance. The first, and most important thing, to know is that insurance is an absolute must. The next thing you need to know is: what kind do you need? This chapter will help you answer this question.

What Should You Insure?

In this creative world, you can buy insurance for just about anything, including flight insurance, credit card insurance, and even pet insurance. As mentioned before, the important question to ask is: what insurance do you really need?

If you purchase a CD player, you can also purchase an extended warranty – an insurance policy that will replace the CD player if anything should happen to it within, say, 90 days of purchase. Is this a serious financial loss? Not really. Electronic stuff that doesn't work after you've spent your hard-earned money on it is definitely an irritation, but it isn't a serious setback.

However, if you're in a car accident and wind up in the hospital for three months and aren't able to work and pay your bills, that is a serious financial loss. Not only are you not able to earn your paycheck, but you've also got hospital bills to pay. This is obviously much more serious than a non-functioning CD player.

As a recent college graduate, chances are you probably need four or five types of insurance. These include:

- Auto Insurance
- Health Insurance
- Life Insurance

- Home Owners/Renter's Insurance
- Disability Insurance

Shopping For The Right Insurance Provider

You've just read the list of insurance coverage you probably need and are thinking to yourself, "If I have to have all this insurance, I'm not going to be able to afford pizza every Friday!" Actually, if you do your homework, purchasing the correct insurance coverage isn't that expensive. The place to start is by choosing the right insurance provider.

Know Your Insurance Terms

Like most industries, insurance has its own terminology. Before you start shopping around, you'll want to know these terms:

- **Premium** – The fee you pay for coverage, usually assessed annually or semiannually.

- **Deductible** – The amount of money you have to pay on a claim before the insurance kicks in. The higher the deductible, the lower the premium.

- **Guaranteed Renewable** – Provision that guarantees that the policy is renewable as long as premiums are paid on time.

- **Co-Insurance** – In health insurance, the percentage of each claim the insured *(that's you)* has to pay over and above the deductible.

- **Co-Payment** – The amount you pay each time you see your health care provider.

- **Lifetime Maximum** – The most a policy *(usually health insurance)* will pay over the lifetime of the policy, or your life.

- **Rider** – Provision attached to a policy that adds benefits not found in the original policy, or that changes the original policy.

- **Beneficiary** – An individual designated in a will to receive an inheritance, or the individual designated to receive the proceeds of an insurance policy, retirement account, trust, or other asset.

Of course, there are many more terms associated with insurance policies. As you evaluate different policies, be sure you understand all the terms included. If you don't know what something means – ask!

Price Isn't The Only Consideration

Price is clearly an important consideration when choosing an insurance provider, but you also need to consider service and financial stability. It won't do you much good if you buy insurance from a company that subsequently goes bankrupt and can't provide you service when you need it. These resources will be helpful as you shop for insurance providers:

- **Publications** – Various independent publications such as Consumer Reports, Kiplinger and Money magazines publish surveys that compare insurance providers' services. You can find these surveys at your local library, or you can pay a small fee to access these surveys online.

- **Associations/Consumer Groups** – There are several associations and consumer groups that produce reports that rate insurance providers. Examples include A.M. Best www.ambest.com, the Insurance Information Institute www.iii.org or the National Association of Insurance Commissioners www.naic.org.

- **Internet** – If you Google insurance you get about 121,000,000 hits. A bit of refined surfing can yield a bounty of information on insurance providers.

Compare Options From Various Insurance Outlets

You can purchase insurance from a number of different types of insurance outlets. Provided below are short descriptions of each of these types. Although one type may seem better for you than the others, it's worth your time to compare all the options.

- **Captive Agents** – The big companies *(Metropolitan Life, State Farm, Blue Cross, etc.)* have agents who work solely for them and will be delighted to sell you any kind of policy you want. Although they only represent options available from their company, they sometimes offer very attractive policies. For example, they may offer extremely competitive rates on auto insurance with hopes of selling other kinds of insurance to you.

- **Independent Agents** – Unlike captive agents, independent agents aren't tied to a particular company. Instead, they represent a variety of insurance companies and plans. Generally, an independent agent will help you shop around for the best deal. They're also well versed in the different types of coverage, so an independent agent might be a great person to have on your team. However, like captive agents, independent agents earn their living on commissions. Therefore, just because they may tout themselves as independent agents, they may be tempted to push certain types of insurance options over other options because of the commissions they can receive.

- **Companies That Sell Direct To Customers** – Some companies sell directly to individuals. Geico is a good example of a large company that doesn't use captive agents. These companies can sell insurance for less because they don't have to pay commissions to either captive agents or independent agents. But they still represent only one company's products, so do your homework.

- **Companies That Shop For You** – There are a number of toll-free phone services and Web sites that will search insurance databases and provide you free lists of the least expensive insurance policies (*similar to how popular travel Web sites work*). Although they offer services similar to those provided by independent agents, they often have access to many more policy options.

Take Advantage Of Employer-Provided Insurance

Many employers offer their employees various forms of insurance coverage, like health, life and disability. In addition, employers may offer some pre-tax insurance options, like flexible spending accounts. The type and amount of insurance coverage offered varies from company to company.

Although the insurance provider or coverage options your company offers may not be your first choice, often the savings are significant. Talk to your employer's Human Resources Department and determine what types of insurance coverage you are eligible to receive. If you require additional or different coverage, use the information provided in this chapter to guide you through the process.

Auto Insurance

Notice that this section does not start with the question: Do you need automobile insurance? That's because unless you are marooned on a desert island somewhere, or you don't own a car, motorcycle or other motor-powered conveyance, you need it.

Like other insurance coverage, auto insurance exists primarily to protect you from financial wipe-out in a worst-case scenario. When you consider that your car is not only a large capital investment, but also more than a ton of heavy metal rushing down the highway, you can see that liability and damage issues could easily be just miles down the road.

All 50 states require a car owner to have automobile liability insurance. Does this mean that all car owners are insured? No. Lots of people drive around without insurance. Statistically, uninsured drivers have little income and few assets for you to tap into in case of an accident. Think about Murphy's Law: Who is most likely to smash into you – the Lexus-owning CEO multimillionaire with a heart of gold and sense of fairness, or the guy who drives a junker he doesn't care about insurance? Exactly.

There are four basic components to automobile insurance. You need to understand them all. Plus, you should know about some of the add-ons. Have your insurance agent explain these categories to you in depth. In most cases, you will be paying for this stuff for years, so you'd best understand what you're paying for.

- **Liability** – Possibly the most important component in the automobile insurance package, liability insurance protects you from costly lawsuits and judgments. Accidents can happen. Often fault is not cut-and-dried, and you may be judged at fault even if you disagree vehemently. Moreover, the other driver may be uninsured or underinsured, leaving you stuck with the bills. The problem is compounded if there are passengers and injuries, or worse. Most states require a specific minimum amount of liability, but you need it even if your state does not require it. There are two components of liability insurance:

  Bodily Injury – Covers the medical costs to those injured other than yourself when you are at fault. There is no deductible for this part of the coverage. Most states require a minimum amount of coverage, but you should talk over your needs with your insurance agent, and insure yourself to the maximum level you can reasonably afford. Increased coverage is not usually terribly expensive. This is definitely a "better safe than sorry" category of coverage.

  Property Damage – Covers the costs to repair damaged property. This can include other vehicles, roadway signs and structures, buildings, or personal property in the vehicles involved. This area

When evaluating auto insurance policies, you will see coverage presented in a format like: 100/300/50. What do all those numbers mean? Well, they describe your monetary limits per accident and per person. In this example, those particular numbers would mean that you have $100,000 in bodily injury coverage per person, $300,000 in bodily injury per accident, and $50,000 coverage for property damage. In other words, if you are traveling with five passengers and you have a bad accident, you will max out at $300,000 for the medical expenses, no matter how injured your passengers are. These amounts can be raised or lowered according to your personal finances and circumstances. Ask your agent or financial planner how much you should carry.

is less fraught with financial peril, but nothing is cheap these days, so be sure you have sufficient coverage.

- **Medical Payments** – This covers the driver and passengers' bodily injury expenses, regardless of who is at fault. Also covered are injuries you may suffer when riding in or driving another person's car. Be sure to ask about single-policy limits, which may be applied on a per person/per accident basis.

- **Uninsured/Underinsured Motorist Liability** – As previously discussed, many accidents involve at least one uninsured or underinsured driver. You need insurance to cover your own lost wages, medical expenses and property damage. While your health insurance may cover your injuries, if you want to protect your passengers, look into this coverage, which usually isn't expensive.

Remember that no insurance company will spend more on your car than its fair market value, usually determined by a blue book chart. A car is "totaled" when the insurance company pays you its value, but it cannot be fixed for that amount. Sentiment counts for nothing. If you are driving your favorite cousin's beloved old red bomb and you wreck it, don't expect your insurance company's heart to bleed for you. Blue book is blue book.

- **Collision and Comprehensive** – Collision and comprehensive coverage are options not every driver needs. Older cars may not be worth the expense of these options, particularly if you carry a high deductible. On the other hand, if you have splurged for a high-end car with a sizeable blue book or fair market value, by all means, consider these types of coverage. Just keep in mind they are not cheap.

> *Collision* – Covers damage to your car that results from a driving accident, whether or not you are at fault.

> *Comprehensive* – Covers non-collision damage, such as hail damage, a tree falling on your car, a window broken by vandals, etc.

Common Questions

What if I lend my car to a friend and he/she has an accident?
Usually, insurance runs with the car. That is, your friend is insured under your policy while driving your car. However, if your friend drives your car to work every day, and you haven't told your insurance company, they may deny you coverage for the accident.

Am I covered by my insurance while driving a friend's car?
The same applies in reverse to this scenario. If you smash up your friend's

car, his/her insurance will cover it, unless the other driver is at fault and can pay. However, if the accident is your fault and you have your own insurance, your friend's insurance company will likely make a claim for reimbursement against your insurance.

Car rental companies tack on fees for "insurance." Should I accept or decline this coverage?
This is not a simple question. If you have opted for comprehensive and collision coverage, your insurance should pay for damages to the rental car, and you simply get to pay your deductible. If you do not have this coverage, then accept the rental company's insurance coverage. Likewise, if you do not have any (*or adequate*) liability coverage of your own, by all means accept theirs.

Health Insurance

Health insurance isn't cheap, but you need it. Even if you are young and healthy, you need health insurance. Consider what would happen if you got really sick and had to spend a week or more in the hospital, or needed surgery and medications. If you do not have health insurance such a situation could literally wipe out any savings you have and possibly put you deep in debt. Hospitals generally don't refuse care for uninsured patients, but they don't treat people for free either.

If you've just graduated from college, here are some coverage options to consider until you get a job that offers health care benefits:

COBRA
COBRA stands for the Consolidated Omnibus Budget Reconciliation Act, and guarantees that workers can maintain their health insurance when they leave a job, but it also applies to college students. If you've been covered under your parents' policy, you can keep that coverage for up to 18 months – if you pay the premiums, plus an administrative charge, yourself. It's not cheap, but it will keep you covered. Act fast, though, since you typically only have just 60 days after graduation to apply.

University Health Plan
If you have been participating in your college's health care plan, you can extend this coverage as well. Check with your college, but be prepared to pay higher premiums. The good news is you'll be able to keep your current doctors. The bad news is the extension may last only a few months.

Short-Term Policy
This policy is just what it sounds like – short-term coverage for a limited period of time, typically one to six months. Usually a short-term policy is

cheaper than COBRA or the university plan. However, keep in mind that short-term policies:

- Do not usually cover pre-existing conditions.
- Are specifically designed to cover unexpected events.
- Typically do not cover preventative care, physicals, immunizations, dental, or vision care.

However you decide to proceed, you need to cover yourself between graduation and that first, benefit-laden job. After you get that job, you still need to look at options. If your employer offers health coverage, take it. If you belong to a union, you'll have access to coverage. You'll probably have to share the cost of the monthly premium with your employer, but it'll be much less expensive than buying it on your own. Sometimes health insurance doesn't take effect until you've been working for several months, in which case a short-term "gap" policy is a good idea. If your employer doesn't provide health benefits, then it's your responsibility to protect yourself.

Primary Types of Health Insurance

The days when insurance programs allowed customers to go to any doctor or hospital they wanted and the insurance company paid 80 to 100 percent of the expense (*fee-for-service plans*), are now few and far between. Now the trend is toward managed-care plans. These types of programs were developed as a means to provide health care through the coordination and arrangement of health services. Because of how managed-care plans are administered, they tend to be the most economical. However, in some cases, options for care are limited. Following are descriptions of a few of the more common managed health care plans.

• **Health Maintenance Organizations (HMOs)** – HMOs are a managed care plan that provides health care through a network of doctors, hospitals and medical professionals. Participants and/or their employers pay a monthly premium in exchange for the HMO providing comprehensive care. Generally, participants cannot seek care from physicians outside of the plan's network unless they are willing to pay for the service themselves. The only way participants can visit an outside physician and have the expense covered by their insurance is to have their HMO approve the visit.

Advantages include:

- No deductibles
- Low premiums
- Minimal out-of-pocket expenses

- Minimal paperwork processing
- Plans focus on wellness and preventative care (*office visits, immunizations, physicals, etc.*)

Disadvantages include:

- Participants must choose a primary care physician (PCP)
- Restricted amount of physicians from which to select
- Referrals from your PCP are required in order to have a visit to a specialist covered by your insurance.

•**Preferred Provider Organizations (PPOs)** – Considerably different than an HMO, PPO participants do not need to designate a PCP, and they can visit a specialist at any time without referrals. In general, for a managed care plan, PPOs are the most flexible, but that flexibility may come at a higher cost to you.

Advantages include:

- Choice of health care providers
- Financial incentives for visiting physicians from the plan's preferred provider network
- Access to any specialist

Disadvantages include:

- The hassle of dealing with reimbursement claim forms, particularly if you choose not to use a preferred provider
- You may be required to pay a deductible
- Premiums are higher than those of other managed care plans.

• **Hybrid, or Point-Of-Service (POS) Plans** – POS is a managed care plan that allows members to see providers outside of the network of preferred providers, usually at a slightly higher co-payment or deductible cost. Although a POS plan is more flexible than an HMO, it also requires participants to select a primary care physician.

Advantages include:

- No deductible
- Out-of-pocket expenses are limited
- Smaller co-payments
- Ability to visit out-of-network physicians

Disadvantages include:

- You must select a PCP
- Considerable co-payments or deductibles for non-network care

Prescription Drug Plans, Dental Benefits and Vision Benefits

These programs are not always provided by traditional health insurance plans, but sometimes your employer will offer these as an extra benefit of working for the company. If your employer offers these programs, take the time to understand how the program works and know what your responsibilities will be if you choose to participate. Some plans may require you to meet a deductible amount before you can receive any benefits. In addition, some plans may limit which doctors you can visit.

Health Care Flexible Spending Accounts (FSAs)

If your employer offers you the ability to participate in a Health Care FSA, consider doing so. An FSA is an attractive way to pay for your health care over the course of a year – with before-tax dollars. How much you can contribute to an FSA will depend on your salary and your employer's policy, but contributions are deducted from your salary before taxes are figured – so your taxable salary is lowered, and so are your taxes. As you incur health-related expenses not covered by your insurance program, you report those expenses to your FSA. Soon after, a reimbursement for those expenses is sent to you.

Keep in mind that the funds you contribute to an FSA must be used in the year you contribute to the FSA. The funds don't carry over year-to-year. In addition, if you don't use all the funds you contribute to the FSA in that year, you will lose that money. Therefore, select a contribution level you are certain you will use in that year.

Medical Spending Accounts (MSAs)

MSAs are a variation on FSAs for self-employed people or people who work for companies with fewer than 50 employees. It works the same way as an FSA, but at the end of the year you can take the unspent money and put it in an interest-bearing account where it will continue to grow – tax-deferred – until you retire. The IRS has loads of information on MSAs on the Web at www.irs.gov.

What Happens To Your Insurance Coverage If You Lose Your Job?

As mentioned before, COBRA requires employers to offer their employees the opportunity to extend their coverage for up to 18 months after employment. Of course, your ex-employer isn't going to pay any of the expenses related to this coverage, so you shoulder the whole cost. But this option is still less expensive than buying your own health insurance.

What If You Don't Have Coverage Through Work?

If your employer doesn't offer health insurance, or if you aren't employed, or if you're self-employed, you still need coverage. Fortunately, you do have some options:

- One choice is to buy an individual policy. Most major insurance companies will sell these, but the cost is substantial.

- If you belong to organizations, sororities or fraternities, or are a member of professional organizations, you may be eligible for coverage through these groups. Most group policies are more affordable than going it alone.

- If you simply can't afford a comprehensive policy, you might want to consider a catastrophic policy. The name pretty much describes what it covers – catastrophic care only. These policies cost much less than full-coverage types. If you're in excellent health, this type of coverage is better than nothing – but not much. Generally speaking, catastrophic plans cover hospital stays. But doctors' services, which are usually billed separately, are not covered. Your room and food – not inconsiderable costs – will be paid, but the rest is yours.

Life Insurance

Do you need life insurance? The answer is maybe. If you are single and have no dependents – and by that we mean no one who formally or informally relies on you for financial contribution – and you or your immediate family have the means to provide an appropriate funeral or other disposition then, no, you do not need life insurance. But keep an eye on this situation, because it's likely to change. If you marry, have a child, become a mainstay to your elderly parent's care or well being, or experience any other of the life-changing events that create responsibility for you then, yes, you need life insurance.

What Are You Protecting When You Purchase Life Insurance?

That is simple: your current income. Those of us who are not born independently wealthy rely on our paychecks to live. Stop and consider what would happen if that paycheck suddenly wasn't there. Most of us would run rather quickly through savings, and wind up at square one as far as personal finances. You want insurance to protect your spouse and/or kids, or your parents or siblings if they rely on you for financial assistance. Life insurance assures that there is money that can be invested or, in some cases, paid out in monthly sums, to produce an income stream sufficient to provide for your loved ones.

How Much Life Insurance Do You Need?

It's a good question but, like all good questions, it has a complicated answer. Since your goal is to provide income to your beneficiaries, you need to do some serious number crunching to come up with an adequate figure. This is a highly personalized calculation, depending on a number of factors, such as:

- Your current income, adjusted for future inflation.
- Your spouse's income and employment options.
- The amount of Social Security your spouse and children can expect to receive.
- The amount of savings you already have.
- The amount of debt you are carrying.
- How old your children are and whether they have special needs.
- Your usual living expenses.
- How much your family's medical needs usually cost.

There are helpful charts available in books and online that let you plug in these numbers and work up a family profile. After you have done that, run your numbers by your spouse, a sensible friend or two, and several life insurance agents. This sounds complicated and time-consuming, and it is, but don't let your loved ones down. After doing this homework, you should arrive at a ballpark number that reflects the amount of income you need to replace, and how much life insurance you need to reach that number. Purchase this amount of life insurance and review your financial position at least once a year to determine if your policy is sufficient.

Life Insurance Riders

Life insurance companies are always coming up with bells and whistles called riders to add on to policies and increase your premiums. Most of these are sheer nonsense, or at least expensive and unnecessary. For example, it is hardly necessary to opt for extra coverage for death by plane. Statistically, that is highly unlikely, unless you are a very careless stunt flyer. Check out these riders carefully. Most cover you for things that you may already be covered for in your existing life insurance policy.

Term Life vs. Cash Value Policies

There are two basic types of life insurance policies: term life and cash value. These go by different names from time to time, but the basic premise is always the same.

- **Term Life Policy** – With term life, you pay the premium and, if you die while you are still actively covered, the insurance company pays the stated insured amount to your listed beneficiary. There is no penalty for canceling the policy.

- **Cash Value Policy** – With a cash value policy – which is a catch-all name for several varieties including whole life, universal life, and variable life – words like "investment" start getting thrown around. You are enticed by the concept that the premiums you pay go into an investment account with your name on it, which will pay a certain amount on a certain day, whether you are alive or dead. Think hard about what you really need and what you are really paying for. Chances are, the cash value is not a good choice for you because, in most cases, it's a savings account/insurance combo that requires you to pay in very high premiums without a comparable yield. The premium is divided into several parts:

  —The amount that goes toward the insurance.

  —The amount taken out in administrative fees and agent commission (*which is much higher than it is for a term life policy*).

  —The amount that gets invested in an account for you.

Moreover, if you cancel a cash value policy before its time, you'll lose a great deal of its value, while the insurance company pockets the windfall. You are much better off in the long run with term life for a low premium and investing the difference in a good savings or investment plan.

Why Get Life Insurance Now?
Besides the fact your dependents are counting on you to provide for them, life insurance is relatively inexpensive and easy to get when you are young. This makes sense when you look at statistics or actuarial tables. A 20-something in good health has a much longer life expectancy than a 60-something also in good health, which means less risk for the insurance company.

Employer-Provided Life Insurance
If your employer offers a life insurance program, by all means take it if it doesn't cost you anything. Otherwise, examine its terms, provisions and options to determine if it's the best policy for you. In some cases you may be able to get a better deal on your own.

Non-Cancelable/Guaranteed Renewable Policies
When shopping for life insurance, you will also want to look for a non-cancelable or guaranteed renewable policy. These policies ensure that you cannot be dropped for "iffy" health once you are covered. Any policy that

requires an annual physical to continue coverage is counter-productive for you.

How Long Do You Need Life Insurance?

You probably don't need life insurance forever. It is, of course, in the insurance company's best interests to get you off their books by the time you are old and likely to cash in your chips. Most people drop their term policies when they can comfortably do so in their later years. This, of course, is a personal decision that should be talked over with your spouse and financial advisor. And your circumstances may require different analysis if, for example, you have a disabled, dependent spouse, adult child or sibling.

Homeowner's Insurance

You've just found your dream home, you've made an offer and the seller has accepted it. Congratulations! Now you need to look into homeowner's insurance. Most mortgage lenders require you to have this, but it's a wise investment anyway because it covers the loss of the house itself and the contents in it. It also provides for some liability insurance protection.

By now you're pretty adept at comparing policies from different companies. You've navigated auto insurance and health insurance. Homeowner's insurance is equally important and at least as complex. With homeowner's insurance, you need to consider not just what the policy will cost, but what kind of policy is right for your circumstances. Policies are based on a variety of risk factors including:

- Your age.
- The age of your house.
- The materials from which your house is constructed.
- The present condition of your home.
- Proximity to fire hydrants and the firehouse.
- Whether there's a burglar alarm system and smoke detectors.
- What potential liability risks there may be, like a swimming pool or pets.
- Your creditworthiness.

Replacement of Structure Coverage

Probably the most important component of homeowner's insurance is the insurance that will cover the cost of replacing the structure itself. To ensure you have sufficient insurance coverage to replace your structure is to determine the true value (*the replacement cost*). You can do this by contacting a builder or a contractor and have them give you an estimate. If you own a new house, you should be able to contact the builder and ask them for the estimate.

When you shop for a policy, be sure that you have a guaranteed replacement cost provision, which means the insurance company will rebuild the home even if the cost exceeds the policy coverage. Also, be sure you understand what the insurance company means by replacement cost, as the description can vary from company to company.

Personal Property Coverage

Another important component of homeowner's insurance is personal property coverage. To determine how much coverage you need, you will need an inventory of the contents of the house. Trek through the house with a clipboard and a pen, writing down everything, or you can take your camera (*video or otherwise*) and take pictures of everything. This is a really good idea because if you ever need to replace something, you've got a visual record of what it looked like.

If you have electronics and computer equipment, be sure you have a record of serial numbers and model numbers as well. Taking an inventory will help you estimate the replacement cost of your possessions, and not just the current cash value. Homeowner's policies generally set personal property coverage at 50 to 75 percent of the structure replacement coverage. This is usually adequate to cover your possessions. If you have unusual items like original art or expensive jewelry, you may want to think about purchasing additional insurance coverage for these items.

Liability Coverage

Liability coverage protects you from possible lawsuits – lawsuits brought because of things that might happen to other people while they're in your house or on your property. Accidents, injury, and property damage are possible lawsuits waiting to happen. Therefore, be sure you have adequate liability insurance to protect your assets from possible lawsuits. You may want to consult a financial planner to determine the amount of liability coverage you need.

What Your Homeowner's Policy Doesn't Cover

Homeowner's policies cover a lot, but they typically do not cover things like:

- Flood
- Earthquake
- Acts of God
- Acts of War/Terrorism

If any of these should occur to your home, you'd be out a substantial amount of cash. Although coverage for these can be expensive, if you are in a high-risk area, purchasing insurance policies for them is probably a wise investment. Contact your state or county officials to determine if your home is located in a high-risk area. To find out if you live in a potential flood area, you can also visit www.fema.gov.

Renter's Insurance

It's estimated that over 70 percent of renters in the United States do not have renter's insurance. They ought to. Renter's insurance works like homeowner's insurance, except that it doesn't cover the structure itself – that's the landlord's problem. All it takes is one fire, or a successful burglar, and you're suddenly faced with a serious financial crisis. Even if you have a furnished apartment, your stuff – like computers, CDs, electronics and whatnot – are your responsibility, not your landlord's.

Renter's insurance is the solution to a lot of your (*potential*) worries. And best of all, it's relatively inexpensive. If you have irreplaceable items like original art, antiques, or jewelry, it will cost a little more – but your peace of mind is worth the investment.

An additional benefit of renter's insurance is the liability coverage that usually comes with it. As we've said before, liability insurance covers injuries that happen to others in your place, and will help out in case of a lawsuit.

Disability Insurance

Disability insurance is sort of like life insurance, only you don't have to die for benefits to be paid. That's a good thing. Disability is just what it sounds like – cash payments that make up for your lost salary if you become disabled and cannot work.

Having said that, don't go overboard with your expectations. Most disability policies are rather stringently written, and few will put you exactly where you were financially, unless you are willing to pay very high premiums. And even then there will be waiting periods and stringent medical proof required.

If you live off of your earned income, and your spouse or life partner does not earn enough to financially support you both long-term, then you need disability insurance. Many experts consider disability insurance more important than life insurance. Why is that?

- A 30-year-old, otherwise healthy man is statistically more likely to be disabled than dead before he's 65.

- Over a third of all disabilities are incurred by those under 45, and most are caused by unpredictable accidents, not medical conditions.

- Moreover, disability insurance, unlike life insurance, provides a benefit directly to you, so even single people with no dependents benefit from, and probably need this coverage.

There Are Two Primary Types of Disability Insurance:

- **Short-Term Disability** – covers a stated percentage of your salary if you are disabled for more than a few days. If you are covered through your job, you usually must exhaust your sick leave first. Short-term coverage is limited in duration of benefits (*often it stops after six months*) and you are unlikely to receive your full salary. If you are employed full-time with a large company, you may have other options. Check with your employer's human resources department to determine what options you are eligible for.

- **Long-Term Disability** – protects you against more catastrophic occurrences. Some policies only cover you for a stated period of time, usually five or 10 years. The better policies will pay you benefits until you are 65. Note, however, that your disability must continue, and you will be required to provide your insurance provider periodic medical updates to verify your condition.

Other Sources of Disability Insurance Include:

- **Workers' Compensation** – is provided by the state government, but in order for you to receive this coverage, injuries must be sustained at work or on company time while performing company work. Benefits are limited, and vary from state to state.

- **Social Security Disability** – is also available, but not easy to tap into. You must have enough work history to qualify, your inability to work must be over a year in duration and, most importantly, your disability must render you incapable of holding a regular job.

- **Your Automobile Insurance** – may give you some disability payments if, of course, your disability is the result of a vehicular accident.

• **Your** Health Insurance – should cover a good bit of your medical expenses. However, chances are it won't compensate you for lost wages.

How and Where Do You Get Disability Coverage?

If you work for a company that offers disability insurance as part of your benefits package, there's no reason not to accept as much coverage as you can possibly afford, and thank your lucky stars. If you work for a company that doesn't offer it, or you are self-employed, explore any options you have that will provide you with some sort of group coverage, which can be considerably cheaper than an individual policy. Professional associations and unions are a good source of group coverage.

How Much Coverage Do You Need?

How much disability coverage you need and what you can afford may not be the same number. Your goal is to get coverage that is as close as you can to the monthly payment that will match what you are taking home now. You cannot insure yourself for more money than you earn now, nor do you qualify for disability insurance if you are unemployed. Disability benefits are not taxed if you pay the premiums yourself with after-tax dollars, but they are taxable to you if your employer pays the premiums. Therefore, be sure to factor this into your calculations. If you have a well-paid spouse, or substantial savings, you may not need as much coverage. Still, be aware that some disabilities result in significant, long-term medical costs that could exceed your health insurance limits.

To determine how much disability insurance you need, take a look at your monthly take-home pay, after taxes and other deductions. Disability payments are quoted to you as a specific benefit per month, so that's the number you are looking for. Note that most employer-offered policies will only give you a certain percentage of your monthly pay. However, this may not be sufficient. If that is the case, see if they offer you the option of upping the coverage at your own expense, which will likely be cheaper than purchasing it on your own.

What Constitutes Disability?

A good question, and not easy to answer. If you are a freelance aircraft pilot and you lose your sight, you sure can't fly a plane anymore. But some policies are pretty stringent, and won't pay if you can perform some other job. You may wish to look for an own-occupation policy. This will pay benefits if your disability precludes you from performing your usual work, but these policies are not cheap. Somewhat less expensive, and perhaps the best compromise, are policies which pay off when you cannot perform the work for which you are reasonably trained. The cheapest policies will require complete and utter disability before they pay off. But if you opt for one of these and become disabled, you may end up perusing the employment section of the newspaper for a job you can perform with your disability.

What About Exclusions?

Be sure to look at what is excluded in the policy. Exclusions can be quite limiting. Some of the most common disabilities, such as back pain, mental illness, migraines, chronic fatigue syndrome and stress-related disorders are sometimes excluded in the fine print – particularly in policies offered by employers who are looking to cut costs. Note that these, in particular, are subjective in that they are not easy to quantify through cut-and-dried scientific testing.

Reducing The Cost Of Insurance

As you have already figured out, insurance isn't necessarily cheap. However, there are steps you can take to help keep the cost down:

- **Your Credit History** – Yet another reason to strive for good credit. Most insurance companies use your credit history as a guide to determine the likelihood that you will file a claim on your insurance. The worse your credit history, the greater your insurance premium.

- **Increase Your Deductible** – Generally speaking, you should opt for the highest deductible you can afford because it will dramatically lower the premiums you have to pay. Of course, if you choose the $1,500 deductible auto insurance, that means you'll have to pay the first $1,500 of any claim you make, so you need to be sure you've got the savings to cover it.

- **Combine Policies** – If you're buying auto insurance, renter's insurance and health insurance and one company provides all these, ask about discounts available if you buy all three from the same company. Also, if you're still living at home, see if adding yourself to your parents' insurance policy (*especially useful for auto insurance*) will reduce the premium. Make sure mom and dad are fine with this first.

- **Shop Around** – As mentioned earlier in this chapter, be sure to compare different companies' offerings. The more you shop, the more deals you will find.

- **Ask About Discounts** – Discounts are available for things like good grades, taking (*and passing*) a driver safety course, driving a car with airbags and antilock brakes. Don't expect your insurance company to just offer these to you. So be sure to ask for them.

- **Avoid Making Small Claims or Inquiring About Hypothetical Claims** – After you've purchased insurance you can prevent increases in your premiums by avoiding frequent claims. In addition, if you have a question about specific damages or injuries that may or may not be covered by your insurance, contact your insurance provider anonymously. Insurance companies keep a record of your calls and can use your inquiries as justification to cancel your coverage or raise your premiums.

Insurance You Don't Need

Remember your hypothetical CD player, mentioned at the beginning of this chapter? Extended warranties are one kind of insurance you don't need. Insurance is for serious things, not the little stuff. Some kinds of insurance you need to be wary of include:

- **Extended Warranty and Repair Plans** – The guy selling you whatever it is has spent a lot of time convincing you it was the best one, the most reliable. Right? So why buy "insurance" to make sure it doesn't break? Just say no.

- **Home Warranty Plans** – If you're buying a house and the seller offers this, take it but don't buy this on your own either. Home warranty plans limit the amount they pay for problems and are generally more hassle than they're worth. You'll have to pay someone to come out and diagnose the problem anyway. Invest that money on a home inspection instead.

- **Dental Insurance** – Unless you've got really bad teeth, these kinds of policies generally cost more than they cover. However, if your employer gives you this kind of coverage, jump on it. Otherwise, pass.

- **Credit Life and Credit Disability Policies** – These kinds of policies show up as offers in your bank and credit card statements. Basically, they pay a small benefit if you die with an outstanding loan (*credit life*) or are disabled and can't work and can't pay the bill (*credit disability*). While they are pitched as a good idea and are generally very inexpensive, the benefits are correspondingly low. When you purchase life insurance or disability insurance, get enough coverage to handle these items.

- **Daily Hospitalization Insurance** – You may not run into this kind of policy since they're usually sold to older people – but just in case you are ever presented with this option, know that what they are offering is to pay a certain amount per day if you are hospitalized – usually in the range of $100 to $150. However, daily hospital charges run in the thousands, so that $100 really covers a very small percentage of the actual costs. Avoid the headache and get a comprehensive health insurance policy instead.

- **Policy Riders** – You will discover that the policies you really need – like auto and disability insurance – come with a long list of add-ons called riders. These include things like towing insurance if your car breaks down. Face it, paying to have your car towed (*and how often do you have to do this?*) isn't that big a financial outlay. Balance the cost per year with what a tow truck would charge you and do the math. You can also buy things like life insurance as an add-on to your auto insurance. Compare the cost of this with the cost of a separate policy and then purchase whatever costs less.

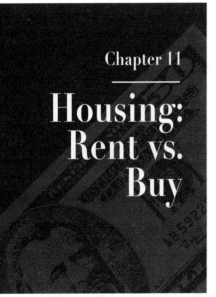

Chapter 11

Housing: Rent vs. Buy

Should you rent or buy? What's the best option? Excellent questions, and the importance of coming up with the right answer cannot be overstated. On the one hand, there is a certain security in renting when your job or salary level is unpredictable, or your personal circumstances are fluid. On the other hand, historically there has been no better place to invest your money than in the American Dream—home ownership. So what should you do?

Although finances play an important role in this decision, a big portion of your final answer will be based on your personal circumstances. This chapter will provide you some useful tools to guide you through the decision-making process. However, keep in mind that your decision should not be taken lightly – or based solely on the content of this chapter. Use this chapter as a companion guide to your own detailed research and analysis. By doing so, you will have the resources necessary to make the right decision.

Rent Or Buy – Which Is Better For You?

To help you answer this question, ask yourself a few basic questions:

- How reliable is my current employment and salary level?

- How predictable are my other personal circumstances, such as my health and my marriage?

- How likely is it that I will want or be able to stay in the same area and house for the next five years?

- How much traveling does my job require? And if I am away a lot, will my spouse, significant other, or roommate be around to handle emergencies?

- How heavy is my current debt load and how well am I managing it?

- How do my annual taxes look, and would the tax deductibility of the mortgage interest be helpful to my bottom line?
- How does my rent compare with a projected monthly mortgage payment, factoring in the tax deductibility?
- How much money do I have in savings, and will it cover a down payment and still leave me with a financial cushion?
- How much responsibility am I comfortable with at this stage in my life?

Before you think about leaving the rental nest and flying on your own, you need to be honest with yourself about the answers to these questions. You also need to consider the advantages and disadvantages of both options.

Advantages of Buying:
- Mortgage interest and property taxes can be deducted from your annual tax return.
- You build equity in your home, both through your monthly principal payment and, more significantly, through the property's appreciation.
- The profits on the sale of your home will likely not be taxed under the home ownership exclusion.
- You won't have to suffer rent increases (*although you are likely to pay increases in property tax, insurance and maintenance/repair costs*).
- In terms of square footage, you will likely get more living space for the money when you buy a home.
- You can refinance whenever interest rates go down, or tap into your home equity with a loan, should you find yourself in need.

Advantages of Renting:
- Instead of needing to come up with a large cash down payment, you can pay down other debt, or invest that money wisely.
- You have no long-term commitment to this living arrangement.
- You don't have to oversee or pay for repairs or maintenance.
- Rent levels may be controlled or regulated where you are, protecting you from burdensome increases.
- You have no obligation to find a new tenant when you are ready to leave.
- You have no risk if housing prices in that area fall.

The relative disadvantages are obvious—the lists are virtual opposites of one another. So, as you can see, there is no clear answer to the rent vs. buy question. The one thing that is clear is that your answer will hinge heavily on your personal circumstances.

The Smart Renter

You've decided that renting is the right choice for you – for now, at least. To ensure that your rental experience is a pleasant one, there are several steps that every smart renter should follow. These include:

Understand the Lease

A lease is a legally binding agreement that will obligate you to pay a specific amount of monthly rent for a specific time period, usually one year. Once you sign it, you will be held to the terms as written. If there are disagreements or conflicts after the lease is signed, the resolutions will be based on the contents of the lease. Therefore, although it may seem tedious to do so, it's important that you read the entire lease document and understand what you are getting into. Also make sure that your lease is in writing. A verbal lease is as legal as a written one, but proving who said what and when is difficult. Pay particular attention to anything the landlord or agent says. If s/he is adding a verbal provision, make

There are all kinds of provisions that creep into leases. If you have a pet, or may want one in the future, watch out for "no pet" provisions or limitations. Look out for cost increases that the landlord is allowed to pass directly to you through surcharges or rent increases. Check out limitations on sublets, roommates, houseguests, or "significant other" sleepovers. Some landlords reserve the right to enter the premises without notice to you, and you may be stuck with this. But make sure they are required to leave notification that they entered, when and why. Look for any provisions that seem burdensome and consider whether you can or should accept it.

sure it gets written down before the final agreement is signed.

If there are any questionable provisions in the lease, check them out with your local or state housing office, or department of consumer affairs. Most jurisdictions have laws on the books to protect renters. For example, understand what, if any, penalties your landlord will charge for a late rent payment. These charges may be set by regulation in your area, and it might pay to know what the law allows. Excessive security deposits may be illegal in your area. Some terms may be difficult for you to meet, and are worth discussing. For example, if the rent must be paid on the 1st of every month, but you are not paid by your employer until the 5th, it may be possible to negotiate the 6th as the day rent is due. You will be more likely to succeed in your negotiating if you are dealing with an individual landlord rather than a large apartment complex, but it's always worth a shot.

Negotiate With the Landlord

Don't walk in and demand a 50 percent reduction – but if a $20.00 per month discount or new linoleum in the kitchen and bathroom will make a difference in your comfort level, it doesn't hurt to ask. In addition, if you have an excellent credit rating, a good, steady job and good references, be sure to remind the landlord of your impressive qualities during the negotiation. A landlord's biggest fear is a poor, non-paying, destructive tenant. If you can reduce any, or all, of these fears, you have a fighting chance to win at the rent negotiation game.

Have Roommates Sign the Lease

If you plan to have roommates, try to get them to sign the lease, or at least be added to it after the fact. This will help to protect you in case one of your roommates causes property damage or walks out on the deal. Sure, the landlord will still hold you and your other roommates liable, but you will at least have legal recourse against the roommate.

Understand Your Obligations Regarding Property Upkeep and Care

Keep the property in good order. If you spot a maintenance problem, call the landlord or property supervisor and report it accurately and promptly. Do whatever you can do to minimize a problem immediately, and don't be a whiner. If you're somewhat handy, offer to fix the little stuff yourself, and keep records and receipts for the work. Don't paint every room a different color, unless you are willing to return the walls to their original paint color before you move out, and you have express permission to do the painting. Anything that you damage or ruin must be replaced or repaired before you leave, so treat the property as if it were your own.

Understand How Your Security Deposit Works

A security deposit is a stated sum, often one or two months' rent, that you pay into an account held by the landlord against any damage you may cause, or rent you fail to pay. Most states have regulations regarding the use of security deposits. Generally, a security deposit cannot be used for basic maintenance. Ask if you can receive interest on the security deposit some landlords will permit this. Make sure you get a written receipt for the security deposit, and, if possible, make the payment by check, with "security deposit" noted on it. Also, it might be a good idea to take pictures of the rental space before you move your stuff in, and after you move stuff out. When you do move out, make sure everything is in good repair, as you found it and, above all, leave the premises clean. Ask for an onsite inspection and written release from your landlord saying everything is in good repair the day you move out. Also be sure to ask when you will get your security deposit back. Most states require security deposits to be refunded within 30 days.

Negotiate New Terms Before Your Lease Expires

Get in touch with your landlord several months ahead of your lease's expiration and try to negotiate improved terms. For example, if you have been a good tenant, see if you can get the security deposit reduced. If you are in a competitive rental market, try to keep your rent at the current rate. Don't wait until the last minute to do this. The more time you have to weigh your options, the better.

Understand Your Rights

As a renter, you have certain rights. Under federal law, the landlord may not discriminate against you based on sex, race, religion or family status. Other things may be regulated as well. For example, if you disregard a provision in your lease, and your landlord is aware of it and accepts your rent anyway, s/he may be precluded from enforcing that provision against you at a later time. Rent increases, too, are often governed by regulation, so be sure you know the maximum annual increase your landlord can impose, and under what circumstances. If you feel there is a problem, find out what local or state agency is in charge of landlord-tenant matters in your area, and contact them as soon as a problem develops.

What Does A Home Cost?

So you think you're ready for the home buying adventure, but you're not quite sure if you can afford it. Following are a number of the most common expenses you will incur when you purchase a home.

- **Down Payment** – is the percentage of the total asking price, in cash, you may be required to pay toward your home. It used to be that 20 percent was required. Now the norm is 10 percent and it can be even lower under certain circumstances. Beware, however, of "zero down payment" loans. They often come with high interest rates or fees attached that don't make sense over the long life of a mortgage. The lender will ask, and you must provide an answer, where the money is coming from. If you are borrowing the down payment, be prepared to explain how you will repay both the down payment and the mortgage. Under certain government-sponsored mortgages, down payments are permitted to be quite minimal.

- **Closing Costs** – are the fees that appear on your settlement sheet. These include things such as the appraisal, notary fees, title insurance, document services, property inspections, and a whole bunch of other stuff. It can all be confusing and can also amount to several thousand dollars *($5,000 to $10,000 is not unreasonable)* out of your pocket at closing – meaning you can't roll these into your mortgage. Ask your mortgage lender at the time you make your application for a good faith estimate of closing costs. In some states, this estimate must be closely adhered to within a small margin, so it is in your best interests to get a copy of the estimate.

- **Principal** – is the amount of money you actually borrow and, therefore, owe.

- **Interest** – is the fee *(expressed as an annual percentage)* the mortgage company charges you to borrow their money.

- **Taxes** – are the fees you pay to your town, city or county. The amount is based on where you live and what your home, and the land it is on, is worth. Contact the tax assessor's office to determine how taxes are calculated.

- **Homeowner's Insurance** – is the fee you pay to an insurance company to replace your home, and belongings, if they are destroyed in a disaster. Most lenders require you to have a homeowner's insurance policy. Homeowner's insurance is not terribly expensive, and is a worthwhile investment. Review the chapter on insurance for more information on this topic.

- **Private Mortgage Insurance (PMI)** – protects the mortgage company if you default on your mortgage. If your down payment is less than 20 percent of the property's appraised value, you will likely be required to purchase private mortgage insurance. When you reach the stage in your mortgage where you do own at least 20 percent of the equity, you should be allowed to cancel this insurance.

- **PITI** – is an acronym for the five terms previously discussed, principal, interest, taxes and insurance. The PITI is an important number, calculated by your lender. It is used to qualify you for a mortgage. The usual formula says that your PITI should not exceed 28 percent of your pre-tax monthly income.

- **Points** – are a percentage fee charged to you by the lender. One point equals 1 percent of the total amount being borrowed *(principal)*. Points are paid upfront, at the signing of the mortgage, and the amount is typically rolled into the total you owe. The number of points you will owe depends on the interest rate and prevailing market conditions. Points can be negotiable, and vary from lender to lender. "Zero point financing" is occasionally available in a sluggish market, but be sure that the interest rate isn't higher, and do the long-term math.

- **Maintenance and Repair** – includes all expenses for the upkeep of your home. This includes everything from maintaining the landscape to fixing leaky faucets. If you're looking to purchase a fixer-upper, be sure to add a significant amount of money to this category.

- **Homeowner's Association (HOA) Fee** – is a fee paid to a fund to cover upkeep of common areas, garbage collection and such things as snow removal. Not all homes belong to a homeowners association, but they are becoming more common. If the home you're thinking about buying does belong to an HOA, be sure your budget allows for annual increases of this fee, as the price for services rise with inflation.

- **Upgrade Expenses** – include all the purchases you anticipate making to get your new home to look nice. This might include new furnishings, window treatments, carpet, that home entertainment center you always dreamed about, as well as home renovations – like a new bathroom or kitchen.

Mortgage Options

If, after you evaluate all the costs associated with homeownership, you are still considering purchasing a home, you will need to understand what mortgage options are available to you. Mortgages are complicated, but millions of people have managed to sort through the options and make wise choices. With a bit of research, and help from your realtor and mortgage broker, you too can find a mortgage option that will best fit your needs. There are two basic types of mortgages:

Fixed-Rate Mortgage
A fixed-rate mortgage is the most common and popular type of mortgage. When a loan agreement is signed, the borrower and the lender have agreed upon the interest rate, which will not change over the entire life of the mortgage, making the monthly principal and interest payments stable and predictable.

For many, many years, almost the only mortgage available to the average homeowner was the 30-year, fixed-rate loan. While that is still the most common type, over the last few decades other mortgage types have become popular, and are offered by most lenders. A 15-year fixed-rate mortgage is exactly like the 30-year, except you pay it off faster. One particular benefit to the 15-year option is that it usually carries a slightly lower interest rate than the 30-year, which means less cost to you. The obvious benefit is that you build up equity much faster, and since the loan is paid off in half the time, the long-term cost to you in interest is much lower.

Adjustable-Rate Mortgage (ARM)

The ARM, also referred to as a variable-rate mortgage, is a term for a mortgage with an interest rate that floats according to what happens to interest rates in the economy. An ARM usually starts off with a "teaser" rate that can be quite attractive. The teaser rate disappears after a stated amount of time—anywhere from three months to ten years, and rates fluctuate from there.

When considering an ARM, look for an ARM with a set limit on how much and how often your rate can be raised, preferably with an annual cap of two points, and one that has a lifetime cap of five to six percentage point over the initial rate. Avoid a pre-payment penalty clause, if possible, since you may wish to refinance an ARM to a fixed-rate mortgage if interest rates drop. ARMs also often have a lock-in provision where, at a certain point, and for a *(hopefully)* reasonable fee, you may lock-in your current rate for the rest of the life of the loan.

Special Programs For New Homebuyers

As a recent graduate, chances are you are a first-time homebuyer. If so, you may be eligible for special state or federal home loan programs. Be sure to ask your lender if you qualify for one of the following programs.

Freddie Mac or Fannie Mae Loan

These are private companies sponsored by the federal government to help expand the mortgage offerings to include all types of borrowers – many who would not qualify for conventional mortgages. Freddie Mac and Fannie Mae do not lend money directly to the consumer, but they do create lending programs that banks and mortgage companies put into effect.

As a rule, the criteria used for mortgages that qualify under these programs are less stringent than the normal mortgage standards, except that you must have a good credit record to qualify. However, your debt ratio can be higher and your income somewhat lower than traditional mortgage requirements. Down payment requirements are lower, too, and not all of the down payment must come from your existing funds—some of it may come from family, friends or foundation gifts. In most major cities, there are no income restrictions for these programs, but they do have caps on loan amounts.

State and Local Housing Authorities

These programs often offer special mortgages for first-time buyers. These are not advertised and not widely known, and terms and requirements vary from state to state. The interest on these loans is often lower than the prevailing rate. Down payments are lower, too, from 0 to 5 percent. There are income level requirements that vary with the local economy. For more information on these programs, contact the National Council of State Housing Agencies at www.ncsha.org.

Federal Housing Administration (FHA)

The FHA sponsors a program that provides mortgage insurance to low-income or first-time buyers. The FHA does not provide the loan itself, but provides federal insurance to the lender in case of default by the borrower. These loans are helpful if you are low on cash, or have poor credit. Your income-to-debt ratio can be higher than that required for a traditional mortgage, and only a small down payment is required—from 3 to 5 percent. Unlike Freddie Mac or Fannie Mae, under FHA you are allowed to add your closing costs to the principal that you initially borrow to complete the sale. On the downside, the FHA mortgage can be more expensive because the federal insurance costs more than private mortgage insurance. But if your credit is iffy and you are short on cash, this may be the best safety net you have to qualify for a mortgage. FHA has no income limits, and maximum loan amounts vary from city to city because of differences in prevailing economies. You can get more information from the Housing and Urban Development office at www.hud.gov.

Department of Veterans Affairs (VA)

If you or your spouse (*provided you are jointly purchasing the home*) have served in the United States armed services, you can qualify for assistance through the VA. Like the FHA, this program does not make the loan itself, but provides partial insurance to participating lenders to help you qualify. The VA usually does not require any set down payment, but the individual lender will have its own requirements. You will pay a one-time charge called a "funding fee," which covers the cost of the insurance. This amount does vary, ranging from 0.5 to 3 percent of the principal amount, depending on the terms of the loan. Eligibility is governed by certain service requirements, and there are no maximum income levels. For more information on this program, contact the VA at www.va.gov.

The Home Buying Process

So you've decided that you're ready to purchase a home. Get some rest now, because you've got a lot of work ahead of you. But don't worry, if you're dedicated and willing to put in the effort, the process can be extremely rewarding. Following are some tips that will make the home-buying process much simpler.

- **Get Copies of Your Credit Report.** Sure, you're positive your credit report is clean, but mistakes can happen – and you wouldn't want a simple error on your credit report to cause your home-buying process to slow down, would you? Take a moment to review the chapter on credit reports. Order your reports and review them. If there are no errors or issues that need to be addressed, then proceed.

- **Shop the Housing Market On Your Own.** Talk to friends, family or co-workers. Identify areas and neighborhoods that fit well with your needs and budget. Spend some time reading the real estate section of your newspaper and scanning the Internet to see what's available. Attend open houses and collect the information that is available on each house. When you tour the houses, pay particular attention to the things you like and the things you don't like. If you aren't going to have much money left over to fix up a house after the purchase, don't buy a fixer-upper. If you discover your tastes and must-haves outstrip your ability to purchase a home, now is a good time to pull back and reevaluate the decision to purchase a home. Start saving your money, and go back to the drawing board on your plans. If, on the other hand, the situation looks do-able, and you've got a good feel for where you want to look and what your style preferences are, it's time to move to the next step.

- **Pre-Qualify For a Loan.** This is a short-cut process that will give you a sense of what size of mortgage you are likely to be able to obtain. By being pre-qualified for a loan, you also look attractive to a seller, and it makes the purchasing a home much simpler.

Note that interest rates fluctuate on a weekly, if not daily, basis. If rates are low when you start the process, try to get your lender to "lock in" the low rate for a certain time *(30-45 days is common)*. This prevents the lender from charging you a higher rate than you were initially quoted at the time of settlement. There is usually a small fee involved and, here, it pays to shop around.

In most cases, pre-qualification can be done over the telephone or Internet. But before you begin contacting mortgage companies do yourself, and them, a favor, and gather the necessary information. The mortgage company will want to know general information about you and your family—names, ages, marital status, age and number of children, and will want a good idea of your professional picture—your and your spouse's salary, employer name and address, job titles, date hired, and if you work on commission or get bonuses during the year. The lender will also want details on your assets, liabilities, and a sense of your current expenses. This is where your net worth statement *(described in chapter three)* will come in very handy.

Pre-qualification doesn't guarantee you a mortgage, but it will give you a comfort level about what you can afford. You must beware, however, that a hungry lender may pre-qualify you for a loan amount that is much larger than you can afford. Don't be tempted by this offer. You know from your budget what you can afford. Use this number as your guide and don't budge from it.

- **Find a Real Estate Agent.** As a first-time buyer, a real estate agent is a must. A licensed, professional real estate agent is trained to work with you, to explore and examine your preferences, to help you to figure out your financial posture, and to find and show you all of the properties that mesh with your heart's desire.

How do you find an agent who's right for you? Start by asking for recommendations from friends, family and co-workers. There are some threshold questions you should ask them:

- Did you like the agents personality?
- Did you feel the agent was knowledgeable about the market in general, and the area in particular?
- Did the agent lack any knowledge you would have found helpful?
- Was it easy to get ahold of the agent when you needed him/her?
- Was the information you got from the agent timely and reliable?
- Did the agent make any mistakes?
- In general, how happy were you with the overall representation and the result?

If you've identified a neighborhood you'd like to live in, drive around and see what agents are listing properties in that area. Do the same with advertisements that focus on the right neighborhoods. Contact these agents, as well as those that were recommended to you, and interview them. Some of the questions you should pose are:

- What is your preferred method of communication, and does that dovetail with mine? (*E-mail, cell phone, regular phone, or a combination of these.*)

- What kind of training have you had?

- How long have you been an agent, and about how many homes do you sell each year?

- How much time can you give me, and do your hours of availability fit with mine?

- How well do you know the area I'm interested in?

- What is the price range you are most comfortable working with?

- Are you comfortable working in my price range, and can you agree not to bother showing me houses that are too expensive for me?

- Can you recommend appraisers, mortgage lenders and home inspectors if I need them and, if you do, will they pay you a referral or finder's fee? Do you have references, preferably from recent clients?

- **Making an Offer**. Once you've found the house you love, you are ready to extend an offer. This is where a real estate agent earns his or her keep. Discuss the size of the offer and the down payment. You should know if the house has been on the market a long time or if it was just listed. Your agent should know if other offers have been made for the property.

If you are just starting out as a first-time buyer, chances are you are not in the market for a multi-million dollar estate. Instead of calling the agent with the biggest, brassiest reputation and advertising cartel in town, why not look for an agent who is, if not a novice, working hard to build up his or her business? S/he might have more time to pay attention to you, and be more willing to work in your price range. Remember that most agents are paid a commission on the sales price of the house, and there is often no correlation to how hard they have to work to sell the most expensive house in town or the least.

When you make your initial offer, be sure to include all the points in it that you feel are important to you. For example, if you are buying a house that is not brand new, you should include a "home inspection" clause, which will let you pay to have the home inspected to determine if there are any obvious or latent defects you should know about. Other contingent clauses may include your ability to finance the loan, a targeted move-in date, or the sale of your present home, if you have one.

When you submit your offer, you will need to write a check for a portion of the down payment – generally less than 2 percent of your offer – called "earnest money" – to show your good-faith desire to purchase the house. This money will be held by the real estate agency in escrow until closing, when it will be applied to the down payment.

Above all, remember that, by law, a contract is a contract. Once all the haggling is done and you have signed an agreement, you will be held to its terms, even if you later decide there's something you forgot, or have changed your mind.

- **Dealing With the Details.** Well before you finalize the purchase of your new home, you should have full approval for the mortgage from your lender. Your lender should provide you with a list of any items or paperwork you are required to bring to the settlement. In addition, between the time your offer is accepted and the time you finalize the purchase of your home, your real estate agent will be assisting you with all the other aspects of your home purchase – including home and termite inspections, radon testing, locating a real estate attorney, etc. This will be a busy time, but keep up the effort – you are almost there.

- **Settlement Day.** Settlement is the process of signing the paperwork (*a lot of paperwork*) and exchanging money (*a lot of money*) for the title to the house.

During the settlement process, you may feel rushed by the parties involved. Don't be. You have put a lot of time, effort, and money into this process, and you want to be sure you understand exactly what is taking place. Allocate sufficient time for this process and ask lots of questions. You want everything to be correct.

Chapter 12

Car: Lease vs. Buy

Purchasing a car is an expensive proposition. And despite all the advertising telling you that you deserve a new car, a car is not an investment. It depreciates, or loses value, over time. Cars, trucks and SUVs lose as much as, or more than, 20 percent of their value the minute you drive it off the lot!

If you paid $15,000 for a new car, after the first 12 months it'll be worth just $12,000. $3,000 dollars vanished. Some models lose as much as 40 percent of their value in the first 12 months. By the time your new car is just four years old it will have lost from 60 to 89 percent of its original value! That $15,000 purchase is now worth a paltry $3,000 to $6,000. In a short four years your car, which is probably still in good shape, has lost $9,000 to $12,000 of value!

If you're following a budget and money is tight, and if you have a reasonably good car already, you'd be better off not venturing into the car leasing/buying process at this time. There are much better uses for your money. In addition, cars on average should last 12 years or 150,000 miles (*or more*) with proper maintenance. In fact, repairing your current car will most likely cost you less than the depreciation on a new car.

However, if you still believe you really need a new car, then proceed with caution. Read this entire chapter before you head off to the dealership. Buying or leasing a car without a plan is like taking an exam without studying – you're doomed to fail, and the consequences can be financially disastrous.

Can You Afford A New Car?

Cars, especially to Americans, represent freedom – freedom to come and go as we please, the freedom of the open road – and for this reason, cars are hugely popular. The problem with cars, other than losing value the minute you drive them off the dealer's lot, is the cost of ownership. That's where your old friend the budget comes in.

The Purchase Price

You've got your budget (*the one you made as you read the Budgeting chapter*) and you're sticking to it, spending within your means. Your first task is to see if you have the money to afford a new car. If you're not paying cash for this car, you need to estimate what the monthly payments might be. One way to do that is to call your bank and ask how much it will lend you to purchase that new car. The answer will depend on a number of factors, like your credit rating and the price of the car. Find out the interest rate you'll be charged and the monthly payment as well. There are a number of Web sites that offer financing calculators that may help you with this process. www. Cars.com is a good one. If the estimated payment you calculated will fit in your budget, that's a start.

The Cost of Ownership

The monthly payment is only one part of buying a car. You need to call your insurance agent and get an estimate of monthly insurance costs on several models you are considering. Add that number to your budget as well. Be sure to include gas, oil changes and other maintenance costs. Then toss in the cost to license it and any additional taxes you may have to pay. Seems like a lot of stuff, right? Absolutely. That's why the decision to lease or buy a car should not be taken lightly.

Now add up all of these expenses. Got a total? Good. Now see if the total cost (*purchase price and ownership expenses*) fits in your budget.

Most people have no idea what the total cost of ownership is for a car, or what they should plan to spend on a car. The general rule of thumb is that your total automobile expense shouldn't exceed 10 to 15 percent of your total monthly budget.

Determining The Car You Need

You will immediately notice that this section is titled "Determining the Car You Need" not "Determining the Car You Want." There is a difference. You may want a new BMW, but what you really need and can afford is a Honda Civic. To help you determine the category of car that fits your needs, complete the following User Profile exercise.

User Profile

Grab a pad of paper. List the following five questions on the left side of the paper and leave enough space for your answers. Ready? Go.

1. How many miles will I drive each year?

If you aren't comfortable guessing, base your answer on how much you use your current car. If you don't have a car, 15,000 miles is a good average.

2. How much time will I spend in the car each day?

You know how long it takes you to get to work if you drive now. If you don't, ask one of your coworkers who drives and lives close to you how much time their commute takes. If you live in a large city, three hours a day wouldn't be outrageous.

3. What kind of driving will I be doing?

15 percent off-road, 35 percent highway, 50 percent city is an example.

4. What is my budget?

Use the numbers you calculated from the previous section. Be sure to include a down payment (*for example, $3,000*) and your total monthly cost over the life of your loan – three years, five years or other.

5. Why do I want and need this car?

This is the most important question, so spend some time on it. Ask yourself "How will I use this car?" and write down the first thing you think of. Keep asking it and writing down your responses. You want a long list here. It might include things like:

- Driving to and from work
- Visiting mom and dad on the weekends
- Taking week-long vacations
- Daily errands, like grocery shopping and taking the dog to the vet
- Taking your daughter and her friends to soccer practice during the week and to games on weekends – need room for equipment

Now review your answers to this question and circle or underline the four most important ones. These four, in most cases, will likely account for 80 percent of the car's use.

Last step.

There are eight different categories of vehicles:

- Sub-compact
- Family sedan or station wagon
- Sports car – sedan/coupe/convertible
- Minivan
- Sport Utility Vehicle
- Pickup truck

- Full-size van or conversion van
- Luxury sedan

Using the four most important uses you identified in question number five, begin crossing out the categories of cars that don't fit these uses. For example, if one of your uses is to haul your children to sports practice, band practice, and all over, then a sports car is simply not practical.

Keep eliminating categories of vehicles until you have only a few left. Then, use the answers to the first four questions in your User Profile to whittle down the list down to the single category that will meet all your needs.

Once you determine the category of car that best meets all of your needs, you can start with the homework. Yes, homework.

Research the different models available in your vehicle category. For example, say you narrowed your search to "family sedan or station wagon." There are not only price levels within the category, but also size segments. Do your homework to determine which price level and size segment meets your needs. Once that is accomplished and you've settled on three models, say: the Volkswagen Passat, the Volvo Station Wagon, and the Dodge Magnum. Now what? More homework.

The good news is there are a lot of resources available – particularly on the Web. Visit the manufacturer's site, as well as third-party sites, and compare features and options on the top three models you've selected. Evaluate safety features and records, automatic or stick shift, cargo capacity, four-wheel drive or all-wheel drive. And, make sure it will fit in your parking space. "Build" the car you want, complete with options. Keep this information. You'll need it when you go for your test drive.

Should You Buy New Or Used?

New cars are definitely nice – nothing can beat the smell of a new car. It's got everything you always wanted and it's all yours. But the used car market has changed in the past 10 years. Because new cars are made better, used cars have higher quality. In addition, as leasing has become more popular, the market has become swamped with two and three year old cars. You simply can't ignore the option of buying "pre-owned." Check out Kelley Blue Book www.kbb.com and Edmunds www.edmunds.com for free access to the current price of almost any used car.

Some online sites – specifically www.autotrader.com and www.cars.com – carry ads for used cars from dealers and individuals. You can see cars available within your zip code, within your state or across the nation – all you have to do is check it out. Anyone who is familiar with eBay knows that eBay Motors offers used cars as well. These sites provide services like used-car inspections to make your experience less of a hassle.

Buying a used vehicle from an individual can be a better deal, financially, but be sure to do the following:

- Make sure the odometer is honest.
- Check the car's accident history. Carfax (*available on the Web or by phone*) will use the Vehicle Identification Number (VIN) and research the history of your car for a small fee.
- Have your mechanic check it out before you buy.

When buying pre-owned, remember that everything is negotiable – except your right to inspect the car. If the seller refuses, walk.

Should You Lease Or Buy?

Leasing a car has become very popular for a number of good reasons:

- It requires little or no money down
- It offers lower monthly payments
- You can drive a better car for less money
- You can get a new car every few years if you want to
- There are no trade-in hassles

But there are disadvantages as well. First and foremost, unless you have a PhD in finance, understanding the terms of the finance charges can be very confusing. On top of that, when the lease is up you give the car back and you have nothing, nada, zilch, zero. You're back where you started, needing a car. Leases also limit the number of miles you can run up on the car – exceed that limit and you owe the leasing company a per mile charge. And should you decide you don't like the car halfway through the lease, you're stuck – or you're going to pay dearly to get out of the lease.

Choosing between leasing and buying is not a simple task, in spite of what the advertising says about leases being simple. They're not. To help you decide which option is best for you, use the following charts. In addition, there are a number of Web sites available that offer advice on leasing vs. purchasing, like www.Cars.com.

The Lease or Buy Comparison Charts

If You	You Should Consider
Typically trade for a new car every 4 years	Leasing
Want to avoid a 10% to 20% down payment	Leasing
Drive 12,000 to 15,000 miles per year	Leasing
Keep your car in excellent condition	Leasing
Don't want to own your car outright	Leasing
Want lower monthly payments	Leasing
Your company will pay for your car	Leasing
You own your own business	Leasing
You want to drive a status symbol	Leasing

If You	You Should Consider
Like to keep a car 5 years of more	Buying
Have enough for a down payment	Buying
Drive more than 15,000 miles per year	Buying
Don't relish paying end-of-lease penalties	Buying
Want to own your own car	Buying
Are hard on your car – lots of wear and tear	Buying
Hate high insurance rates	Buying

What About Your Current Car?

You have basically two options: use your present car as a trade-in or sell it on your own. There are advantages and disadvantages to each option.

Using Your Car as a Trade-In

If you choose this option, the first and most important thing you need to know is what your car is worth. You can check the going value at Kelley Blue Book www.kbb.com, but keep in mind that when you trade, you'll be getting a "wholesale" value and not the retail value. Kelley lists both.

A lot of features go into this value. Some will add value (*air, sunroof, CD player, power windows, etc.*) and some will detract (*high mileage, dull or chipped paint, rust, pitted glass, worn upholstery, etc.*). Consider these before you decide to trade.

Selling Your Car on Your Own

Before you choose this option, ask yourself the following question: Am I a top-notch negotiator? If the answer is no, you'll want to revisit the trade-in option. If you're comfortable negotiating with the people who will come to see – and drive – your car, then go for it.

You'll need to advertise – the local newspaper is filled with ads for owners selling cars. You can also post your offer on the Web. Visit www.autotrader. com and www.cars.com. You can also check out eBay Motors at www.motors. ebay.com.

Then there is the consideration of your time. What is it worth? You have to be home when people come to see the car – if they even show up. You need to deal with the sales paperwork, the title transfer, and whether to take a check from a person you've known for a total of 45 minutes or demand cash. Selling your car yourself is not for the faint of heart or those who lack patience. The upside is you might be able to get a better price for your car.

Preparing For The Test-Drive

At this point you should have narrowed your selection to three models and have a list of specific options you want. Now do some homework on the local dealers that sell those models. Don't worry about price at this point – you just want to test-drive the cars. *You're not buying anything yet!*

It's a good idea to test-drive all three models in a short time period so you have the opportunity to compare the look and feel of each car. Contact each dealership, let them know you'd like to test drive a certain model, and be very specific. You want to drive the car that's equipped exactly the way you want it. If the first dealership doesn't have what you want, don't let them talk you into something – especially over the phone. Simply call the next dealership. If there isn't another dealership in your area, ask when the specific model with the specific features will become available. Another thing: be sure to let the dealer know that you're only interested in test-driving the car, that you'll be test-driving several different models, and that you'll be making your purchase decision only after you've finished all your test-drives.

How To Test-Drive a Car

Show up for the test-drive prepared. Bring a list of the options you want, as well as a list of questions. Bring a notepad to take notes. If someone else (*spouse, friend, child*) will be driving the new car, bring them along as well. Remember, *you're not going to buy anything today!*

When you arrive at the dealership, allow the salesperson to show you the car you asked to test-drive. Have him or her explain all the features. Listen to what the salesperson has to say and ask a lot of questions. Write down all relevant information, including the price listed on the vehicle and any specials or leasing options the salesperson offers. If they present a car that is not what you were intending to test-drive (*such as a completely optioned-out model or similar model*), request that they get a model that meets your specific requirements. You only want to test-drive the specific models you requested in order to conduct a fair comparison. Remember, *you're not going to buy anything today!*

When you test-drive, drive the car in similar situations that you would normally drive – city, highway, etc. If possible, test-drive the car in a familiar area – such as your normal driving route. Also note your "feel" for the car – access to various controls, ease of seat adjustment, where you can store your morning coffee or soda, etc.

After the test drive, leave the dealership. Thank the salesperson for their time and mention that you have another test-drive appointment to get to. Whatever you do, don't talk price or deals. The salesman will try to entice you with special offers available that day only. It's a gimmick. Avoid it. Just get out. Drive somewhere and complete your notes with any final thoughts about the car you just tested and then repeat the entire process for the other models you are considering.

Determining The Price

Once you have done your homework and completed the test-drives, your decision should be becoming clear. If not, determining the price may be helpful. A lot goes into pricing cars, and the Internet is the best place to start gathering this information.

The first price you generally see is the one on the window of the car. This is the infamous Manufacturer's Suggested Retail Price (MSRP). Pay close attention to the second word: "suggested." That means arbitrary. It is a suggestion and has no relationship to what it cost the manufacturer to make the car. Only uninformed buyers negotiate from the MSRP.

Instead, you need the manufacturer's invoice price. This price isn't related to cost either, but it tends to be more realistic. It's what the manufacturer charges the dealership. and it's available to anyone. If you go to almost any Internet car-buying price guide sites (*www.edmunds.com* *is an example*) you can find the invoice price of practically any car. These sites also have the installed-option equipment prices so you'll know what the dealership has to pay for that super-cool 15-disc CD changer you decided you had to have.

Simply add up all the extras and you've got a starting point.

There are a couple of other things you should know before you grab your checkbook and speed over to the dealership to negotiate. These include:

- **Dealer Holdback** – The percentage of the invoice price the manufacturer sets aside for the dealer (*usually 2 to 5 percent*) and then pays the dealer each quarter. Most of the Web sites will have this information.

- **Manufacturer to Dealer Incentive** – The amount the manufacturer offers the dealer to sell the car. Again, most buying guides can help you determine how much this incentive is.

- **Customer Incentives** – These include low finance rates, cash back, and other enticements. Sometimes these have a real value – so be sure to check them out thoroughly.

The final exercise is to calculate the price of your car. First, list the manufacturer's invoice price, add all the options you want, then subtract all incentives (*customer, dealer and holdback*). Add back in the delivery charge (*from the window of the car or one of the Web sites*) and, voila, this is your price. Will the dealer sell the car for this price? Most likely not. But you are in a much better spot to start negotiating than if you had started with the higher MSRP.

Financing Your Purchase

If you are planning to purchase your car instead of leasing it, you should spend some time doing your homework on the various financing options before making an offer on a car. You already talked with your bank and got an estimate. Take the new information you've developed on price and talk to the bank again. Car loans generally come in 36, 48, and 60 month terms, with smaller monthly payments for longer-term loans. Take the shortest-term loan you can manage. If you can afford paying the car off in three years versus five years, do it and pocket the savings.

Historically, dealerships have not offered the most competitive financing options. However, that has changed in recent years. In fact, in some cases dealerships offer the best financing options available. If the dealer you are considering purchasing a car from is offering a better financing option than other sources you have investigated, go with their option.

An alternative to traditional auto loans from the bank is a home equity loan. Why consider using this to purchase a car? Because interest on home equity loans is tax deductible, while interest on your car loan isn't. If you have sufficient equity in your home, consider this option as a means to purchase your car. You can learn more about this option in the Home Equity chapter.

Whichever financing option works best for you:

- Put as much money as you can into the down payment
- Pay off the loan as early as you can
- Pay cash whenever possible

Choosing The Car For You

You should now be in possession of three sheets of paper – one for each car – with:

- The model you test-drove
- The options you chose
- Your comments and thoughts on the car
- The price you calculated from the previous section
- Your decisions on new vs. used vs. leased
- The loan information from your bank
- The total of the other costs of owning a car (*insurance, etc.*)

Spread these sheets out on the table and evaluate all the information and then make your choice.

Purchasing Your Car

Based on all your research, you are now ready to make your purchase. Depending on your comfort level for negotiating, there are several ways to conduct the purchase. If you enjoy the negotiating process, by all means, head to the dealership(s) that are offering the vehicle you have decided upon and start negotiating. But beware! Dealerships conduct negotiations on vehicles every day and are professionals at it.

A better option is to conduct your negotiation process by not ever setting foot on the dealership lot. You read that right. Stay away from the dealership. This puts you in control. Here's how:

- Locate the fax numbers for all the dealers within 100 miles of you that offer your number one choice of cars.

- Create a detailed description of the car you are seeking on a single sheet of paper.
- Create a fax cover sheet that introduces yourself and tells the dealer that you intend to buy a car within a week. This way they'll know you're serious and it puts a time frame around the bidding.
- Personalize the fax if you can by addressing it to the Fleet Manager or House Manager *(call the dealership to get names)*.
- Let them know you'll be taking bids over the next three days.
- Fax the appropriate sheet to the appropriate dealer and sit back and wait.

Some of the responses will be form letters. Set these aside. Wait for the real ones and, when they come in, look at them closely. Be sure they include all the options you asked for. While you may get one amazingly low bid, more than likely you'll get a few that are below the MSRP, but within the range of your calculated price. You may have to send out a second round of faxes asking the dealers to beat your lowest offered price, but at some point you'll need to call the dealer and tell them you'd love to accept their bid.

Sometimes the fax-for-bids method doesn't work. Some car dealers – Saturn, for example – just don't do business that way. If a Saturn is what you decide you want, skip the faxing and just go buy the car. They don't negotiate. If the car you want is a victim of the supply/demand curve – it's in short supply and there's a high demand – the fax strategy won't work. If you don't have at least 10 dealerships bidding against each other, the fax strategy won't work in this case, either. One thing that will work in your favor, though, is to wait until a week before the end of the month. There's always pressure on dealerships to sell a lot of cars at the end of the month.

After you've called the dealership, thanked them for their bid and accepted it, arrange for a time that you can come down to pick up your new car. Check to be sure you have all the features you asked for *(one more time)* and even ask to drive it. Once you're satisfied, sign the papers, take the keys and say "thank you." You're the proud owner of a new car.

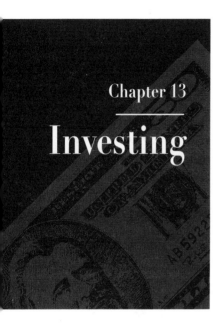

Chapter 13

Investing

Investing frequently scares people – they see it as extremely complex, requiring years of study or a lot of money. And most people don't understand what the purpose of investing is – which is to build wealth. Yes, it can be complex. Yes, you could spend years studying it, but the one thing it doesn't require is a lot of money – as little as $50 or $100 per month will get you started. This chapter will provide you with a basic understanding of investing – what it is and isn't, some guidelines on how to determine your tolerance for risk *(because there is risk involved in investing)*, and a description of the common investment options available to you.

Saving vs. Investing

The terms "savings" and "investing" are frequently used interchangeably, but they are very different.

Saving

Savings are dollars you've put aside for emergencies or for very specific purposes. When you save, you want the money to be there when you need it. Therefore, you need a safe place to keep it. Savings accounts and other low-yield accounts are ideal for savings. Saved dollars are "liquid" dollars – they're available when you need them. You don't have to sell anything or wait to get your money. You go to the bank or other financial institutions, and ask them for your money and they give it to you.

But wait, you're saying. "I get paid interest on my savings. Doesn't that make it an investment?" Not really. Savings accounts are very safe (*low risk*) and don't yield much return – interest-bearing checking and/or savings accounts pay as little as 0.25 percent annually – and some even charge you a fee for managing that savings account. Money market accounts (*a form of savings account*) have slightly higher yields, but generally require you to meet certain requirements to qualify for that extra 0.50 or 0.75 percent.

Investing

Investing is about increasing your net worth, and about meeting long-term financial goals. It involves more risk (*possible loss of money*) than saving, but provides more rewards (*possible greater yield*) as well.

A Word On Inflation

You can spend your life passing money into a savings account and never create wealth. In fact, you may go backwards if inflation is greater than the interest you're earning. Inflation adjusts compared to the status of the economy. For example, say you have $1 in a savings account earning interest at a rate of 2 percent. If inflation is also rising at 2 percent, then that $1 is worth the same amount one year from now as it was when you put the $1 into the savings account. On top of inflation, you are also required to pay income tax on the interest you earn. Therefore, if you want that $1 to grow in value, you need to place it in an account (*an investment*) that will allow it to grow faster than the rate of inflation.

Are You Ready To Start Investing?

Maybe. Maybe not. If you can answer "yes" to the following questions, then you are in a position to start investing. If you answer "no" to any of them, you'd be wise to wait.

Do you have an emergency fund of at least three months' living expenses?
You need this much set aside so you won't have to sell your investments to get through something like the loss of a job or a serious illness. A three-month cushion (*some suggest at least six months*) will see you through most emergencies.

Do you have adequate insurance?
You need health insurance, disability insurance (*especially if you're the primary source of income for your family*), property, auto and liability insurance. Why? To avoid a financial disaster should something happen to you, you cause damages to someone else or their property, or you are sued.

Do you have no credit card or other high-interest debt?
If you're carrying any credit card debt, the best investment you can make is to pay them off! It will do you no good to have investments yielding 8 percent if you're spending more than that to service high-interest debt.

Are you maximizing your retirement options such as your 401(k) or other opportunities?
Plans that provide matching funds are extremely valuable and should be the first on your list of investments to take advantage of. If your employer offers to match a portion of your contributions, for example fifty cents to a dollar for every dollar you contribute, jump at the opportunity. None of the investment choices you'll find out about in this chapter will return that much.

Do you have a budget that you follow?
A well-maintained budget is an important and valuable tool. Not only does it provide you information about how you are spending your money, but it also provides you information about the funds you may have available to invest. Besides, it takes discipline to be a successful investor, and if you have a budget you stick to each month, you've shown you have what it takes to invest.

How did you do? If you answered yes to all of these questions, you have a lot to be proud of. And a lot to look forward to.

What Do You Need To Start Investing?

If you meet the criteria outlined in the previous section, your next step is to determine how much you have to invest and how much you'd be comfortable with investing. You don't need a lot of money to start investing – you just need to start! Look over your budget. If you have as little as $50 a month available, you can start investing.

Two myths about investing:

You need a lot of money to invest.
Not so. For example, most mutual funds require a minimum investment of $2,000 to $3,000. However, some will allow you to open a fund with as little as $50 if you agree to have that amount automatically deposited monthly from your checking account. But mutual funds are not your only option; there are many other investment options you can participate in with a minimal monthly contribution. These, as well as mutual funds, will be described later in this chapter.

You'll need to pay a financial advisor to help you invest.
A lot of investments can be purchased without consulting a financial advisor. You just need to do some research, which is much easier these days because of the Internet. In fact, you can make many of your purchases online as well.

The truth is that investors generally start out small – especially when they're young. The great thing about investing when you're young is that you have the luxury of time – time to watch your tiny investment grow. Be patient, be careful, and you'll have fun watching your investments grow.

How Much Risk Can You Tolerate?

Risk, as it relates to investing, is the possibility that you could lose some or all of your money. Investing isn't exactly like gambling, but you can lose your initial investment all the same. If you understand just how much work it takes to earn a dollar, you also need to understand what your tolerance is for losing some, or all, of that entire dollar.

Assume that you have $1,000 to invest for 12 months. If losing 5 percent of that money, or $50, is the most you would be willing to lose, then you probably have a low risk tolerance. If, on the other hand, you would be okay with losing 25 percent, or $250, count yourself as a moderate risk-taker. If the thought of blowing as much as 40 percent ($400) of your initial $1,000 isn't all that troubling, you likely have a high-risk tolerance.

If You Have	And Could Tolerate Losing	You're A
$1000 to Invest	5% or $50	Low-risk Investor
$1000 to Invest	25% or $250	Moderate-risk Investor
$1000 to Invest	40% or $400	High-risk Investor

Do the same calculations, only this time up the initial investment to $10,000. What's your risk tolerance now? 5 percent ($500)? 25 percent ($2,500)? 40 percent ($4,000)? Your risk profile will change depending on the amount of money you invest, your investment goals, and the circumstances of your life. One way to do that is to understand not only what you want to use your investments for, but also when you want to use them.

When Do You Want To Use Your Investments?

You've already worked on your goals. You understand what savings is for and how it's different from investing. Now take a look at your long-term goals. These are the goals you will use your investments for. For example, planning a wedding, taking a once-in-a-lifetime vacation or owning a dream home – these are goals consistent with investing.

Your timetable will impact your risk profile. Short-term investments – that pending wedding, for example – may require less risky choices because you need the money in, say, a couple of years. As with savings, you want that money available when you need it. Your once-in-a-lifetime vacation might call for a moderate risk strategy because it's farther away. But your dream home? That's going to take a lot of money and a lot more time, so a higher-risk investment might be the right choice. Remember, the higher the risk, the higher the potential reward. What you want to do is strike a balance between wildcat, go-for-broke high-risk investing and ho-hum investing by finding investments that will accumulate wealth and still let you sleep at night.

Retirement, while it seems like it's eons away, might take a completely different strategy. The Securities and Exchange Commission (SEC) suggests that if your investment horizon, or the amount of time you have to let your money accumulate wealth, is long – say 35 or 40 years until retirement – you might consider more risky investments. Why? Because less risky investments may grow too slowly to keep up with inflation. Finally, fees for your investments need to be considered. For example, if you decide to invest, there are usually fees included in the purchase and sale of those investments.

Clearly, before you begin investing you need to think about these factors, as well as your goals, your timeline for achieving them, and your risk tolerance.

What Are Your Investment Options?

The most common choices of where to invest your money include cash, bonds, stocks, and mutual funds. Each of these choices includes a variety of options.

Cash
As mentioned earlier, cash is a form of savings. However, when developing an overall investment plan, it's important to understand what savings options are available to you. Following is a list of common cash savings options.

- **Savings Account** – Savings accounts are usually offered by financial institutions, such as banks, and offer a very low rate of return. Money usually can be withdrawn without penalties.

- **Certificates Of Deposit (CDs)** – CDs are a specialized deposit that can be purchased from a financial institution such as a bank or credit union. A CD is a loan you make to a financial institution over a certain time period. Most CDs provide annual interest payments during the life of the CD and will return the original invested amount plus interest when the CD expires.

  CDs often offer a higher rate of return than savings accounts because of the time requirement involved. However, you should be aware that if you withdraw money from a CD prior to its maturity, you will be assessed a fee for early withdrawal.

- **Money Market Account** – Money market accounts are invested primarily in short-term and high-quality bonds, treasury bills, and CDs. They usually offer returns higher than a savings account, but lower than a CD. The advantage of money market accounts is the ability to withdraw money withouts penalty. Some money market accounts are now insured up to a certain dollar amount. Therefore, prior to investing, determine if the money market account is insured and up to what limit.

Bonds

A bond is an IOU promised by the United States government (*treasury bonds, savings bonds*), federal agencies, state and local governments (*municipal bonds*), and corporations (*corporate bonds*). In return for your loan, the creator of the bond promises to pay you a specified rate of interest during the life of the bond in addition to repaying the entire value of the bond when the bond matures.

Bonds, just like other forms of investments, include several options based on the amount of risk you're willing to accept. The great thing about bonds is that a rating system has been developed to determine the amount of risk associated with a bond. A bond that is rated triple-A (AAA) is usually safer than a bond that is rated double-B (BB). However, the AAA bond will usually have a smaller rate of return than the BB bond. Bond ratings are available from several resources, such as the Internet, financial institutions, and newspapers. Below are descriptions of the various forms of bonds.

- **Treasury Notes and Bonds** – The U.S. Treasury issues treasury notes (*two to ten year maturity*) and treasury bonds (*ten to thirty year maturity*). These investments are backed by the "full faith and credit" of the United States government and thus are considered low risk.

- **Municipal Bonds** – Bonds issued by states and municipalities to finance public projects, such as roads, schools, and hospitals are municipal bonds. One benefit of municipal bonds is that they may be tax-exempt from federal and state taxes.

- **Corporate Bonds** – Occasionally corporations need to borrow money for long-term projects. Instead of issuing more shares of ownership (*stock*) to raise funds, a corporation will issue bonds. The risk associated with bonds will vary on the history and financial stability of the company offering the bond.

Stocks

A stock is a unit of ownership in a corporation that you receive in the form of a piece of paper. The ownership of a stock entitles you to participate in various decision-making matters, such as the election of a company's directors or the sale of additional shares of company stock. By purchasing a share of the company, you are accepting the possibility that the company's value may increase or decrease. This increase or decrease in value will be reflected in the company's stock price.

In addition to the increase or decrease in a company's stock price, some corporations offer their shareholders dividends. Dividends are payments of the company's profits that are not invested in the company. Dividends are most common in very large, low risk, and financially stable companies. Once you purchase stock in a company, you may be able to purchase additional shares of the company's stock with dividend payments. This is known as a dividend reinvestment plan. This lets you gives you obtain more shares in the company while avoiding fees normally associated with purchasing additional shares.

Although there is no mandatory length of time you must retain ownership of stock *(except in specific situations)*, stock tends to be a long-term investment. In addition, the fees associated with the purchase and sale of shares of stock typically make frequent purchases and sales cost-prohibitive.

Listed below are brief descriptions of the categories of company stocks.

- **Large-Cap Stocks** – Stocks offered by large companies, such as automobile manufacturers and utility companies, are known as large-cap stocks or "blue chip" stocks. These shares generally have limited growth prospects, and investments in these companies are usually suited for long-term investment horizons. Although the stock price may remain relatively stable, these companies offer the largest dividends.

- **Mid-Cap Stocks** – Stocks offered by mid-sized companies, such as regional grocery chains, are known as mid-cap stocks. These shares generally have good growth prospects and tend to re-invest profits. Therefore, dividends are rarely offered by these companies.

- **Small-Cap Stocks** – Stocks offered by small companies, such as start-up technology companies, are known as small-cap stocks. These stocks tend to have good growth prospects, but may be based on unproven *(non-stable)* products or services. Therefore, the risk associated with these stocks is quite high. Because these companies are interested in building up their business, profits are almost always re-invested and never paid out as dividends.

Mutual Funds

Mutual funds were developed as an investment tool that gives investors the ability to pool their money together and invest in a variety of assets. Professional money managers invest this money and spread the money among various types of assets. This allows you to spread your funds and risk among many assets that would otherwise be cost prohibitive.

To ensure that the mutual fund is invested in the proper assets that will maximize growth within a certain acceptable risk level, a manager is appointed. All mutual funds charge a fee for this management service. The size of the fee depends on the level of management involvement. Management fees are usually charged as a percentage of the value of your mutual fund. For example, you might be charged 2 percent of the value of the fund.

As with stock, the fees and expenses associated with buying and selling a mutual fund tends to make investing in a mutual fund a long-term investment decision. In addition to the fees and expenses, a longer time frame is needed in order to achieve the intended results.

Following are brief descriptions of the various forms of funds:

- **Money Market Funds** – Money market funds are invested primarily in short-term and high-quality bonds, treasury bills, and CDs. They usually offer returns higher than a savings account but lower than a CD. The advantage of a money market account is the ability to withdraw money without penalty.

- **Bond Funds** – As discussed earlier in this section, there are a variety of bonds available for purchase. Because of this variety, there are a number of options for mutual funds based on bonds. For example, you can have a corporate bond fund, municipal bond fund, or U.S. government fund.

- **Stock Funds** – There are a number of choices of mutual funds that invest in stocks:

    Aggressive Growth Funds – typically invest in small companies and are usually one of the highest-risk mutual funds. These companies almost always focus on growth and do not pay dividends.

    Growth Funds – typically invest in well-established companies that emphasize growth and usually small dividends.

    Growth & Income Funds – typically invest in firms that have some growth potential, but mostly focus on firms that consistently pay dividends.

    Income (Equity) Funds – typically invest in companies that pay dividends.

    Global Funds – typically invest in stocks of overseas companies as well as the United States.

    International Funds – typically invest strictly in stocks of overseas companies.

Set-up and management fees are commonly referred to as load and no-load funds. Below is a brief description of these fees:

- **Load Fund** – A load fund will charge either an up-front fee when the fund is purchased or a redemption fee when the fund is liquidated. For instance, if you have $1,000 to invest in a fund and the fund charges an up-front fee of 3 percent of your initial investment, $30 will be deducted from the $1,000 and the remaining $970 will be invested.

- **No-Load Fund** – A no-load fund will not charge up-front or redemption fees. However, many of these funds tend to charge for a variety of other services. Therefore, be sure all possible fees are explained to you before you agree to a no-load fund.

Diversification

If you know the phrase "don't put all your eggs in one basket," then you know what diversification is. Because investments fluctuate, if you place your money in different investments with returns that are not completely correlated, when some of your investments are down in value, odds are that your other investments are up.

Diversification is one of the reasons mutual funds have become a good choice for investors. As mentioned before, mutual funds give you the ability to purchase a variety of different stocks, bonds, or cash equivalents. If you purchased one of these securities on your own, say stock in General Motors, your success or failure would depend solely on the performance of that individual stock. However, when you invest in a mutual fund, you are investing not only in General Motors, but also dozens or even hundreds of other companies. Thus, if General Motors' stock plummets, chances are the stock prices of all the other companies in your mutual fund will counteract the negative effects of the reduced value of General Motors' stock.

You may be thinking to yourself that in order to further diversify your investments, you should purchase a mutual fund in each of the different investment categories. For example, one in stocks, one in bonds, and one in cash equivalents. This would certainly diversify your investment portfolio. However, you now have several different mutual funds to keep tabs on, plus you're paying management fees to each of these funds. To avoid this hassle and cost, mutual fund companies have created several individual funds that accomplish this for you – where the fund includes a mix of stocks, bonds and cash equivalents. Therefore, you achieve a diversified investment portfolio (*in stocks, bonds and cash equivalents*) with only one mutual fund.

Asset Allocation

Asset allocation is a term used to describe how you spread your money among different investment options (*stocks, bonds, and cash equivalents*). So how do you decide how much of your money should be allocated to stocks, how much to bonds, and how much to cash equivalents? The answer is dependent on a number of factors, including your present financial situation, your goals, and the risks associated with various investment options.

A general rule of thumb is to make sure you have at least three to six months of living expenses in cash equivalents in case of an emergency. Once you accomplish that, take the remaining amount of funds available for investing and allocate that to stocks and bonds. "How much of each?" you ask. A common (*conservative*) approach to asset allocation is to subtract your age from 100 and invest the resulting percentage in stocks. The remaining amount is invested in bonds. For example, if you're 23 years old, you would aim to invest 77 percent (100-23) in stocks and 23 percent in bonds.

Of course, this approach to asset allocation may not fit everyone's specific needs. If you are a moderate or high-risk investor, you may want to allocate more of your money to stocks. Again, this is a personal decision and is dependent on a number of factors. Do your research, consider the risks, and choose wisely.

Which Investments Should You Choose?

When you are ready to start investing, you will soon realize that there are a tremendous amount of investments to choose from. The key is to narrow what you would like to invest in and then research the various options to determine what is the best fit for you.

There are an amazing amount of resources available on investing – everything from books, magazines, Web sites, television shows, investment companies, and financial planners. Utilize all of these resources, ask questions, and do more research. As you know, investing involves risk, and the more you know, the better equipped you are to evaluate that risk.

Where Should You Purchase Your Investments?

There are literally thousands of companies that sell investments – banks, mutual fund companies, securities brokers, and even insurance companies all compete for your investment dollars. The companies you should look for are those that offer you valuable help without charging outrageous fees and those whose representatives have no self-interest in which investments you buy. Like always, research the various options to determine what is the best fit for you. Following are descriptions of a few of the common choices.

Full-Service Broker

Full-service brokers are the middle-person that takes your buy and sell orders and relays them to the market. In addition, full-service brokers give you advice regarding your personal financial planning. This planning will help you set goals, provide you with advice on investing, and help you develop timelines to meet your goals. Keep in mind that this "full-service" comes with a big fee. If you've done your own research, this is a service you probably don't need.

Discount Broker

If you know exactly what investment you wish to purchase, a discount broker may be the way to go. A discount broker will take your buy and sell orders to the market; however, they do not provide any form of advice or financial planning services. Discount broker services can be utilized either in person, via touch-tone phone, telephone with a live person, or via the Internet.

Internet

The Internet provides potential investors with a multitude of choices and information regarding investing. In addition, the Internet offers many investment services at significant discounts. However, be certain you are dealing with a legitimate company before transferring personal funds to them.

Mutual Fund Company

Most mutual fund companies allow customers to purchase a mutual fund directly, thus bypassing the full-service and discount brokers. This method can provide cost savings depending on the type of mutual fund you purchase.

Chapter 14

Retirement

If you think you have plenty of time before you need to start investing in your retirement, think again. It's to your advantage to start now!

You're probably thinking, "Yeah right. I barely have enough to make ends meet as it is. And what's the big hurry anyway? I'm not going to retire for 30 or 40 years. So why worry about this now? Right?" Wrong!

Now is the perfect time to start investing in your future. Why? Because you have 30 to 40 years of time to invest, and time is money. What does this mean? Consider the following example.

Recent Graduate	Not-So-Recent Graduate
• *Begins investing for retirement at age 21.* • *Invests $2,000 each year until she is 29, and does NOT invest any more money for her retirement after that.* • *Total contributions: $18,000 at a 10 percent compounded rate of return.* • *Value at age 65:* **$839,556**	• *Begins investing for retirement at age 30.* • *Invests $2,000 each year, and continues to do so until she is 65.* • *Total contributions: $70,000 at a 10 percent compounded rate of return.* • *Value at age 65:* **$598,253**

As you can see from this example, the difference is significant. In fact, the difference is almost $250,000! Just imagine if our Recent Graduate had continued to invest $2,000 a year into her retirement until she was 65 instead of stopping at age 29. The difference would be astronomical.

Compounding interest over time puts your money to work for you. A little effort early on in your life will reap large rewards in your future. Don't put investing in your retirement off until it's more convenient. You can't afford to.

How Much Money Do You Need To Retire?

This is a tricky question. The general rule used to be that an upper-middle class couple needed about $1 million in assets to maintain a comfortable retirement. However, when you consider inflation and the fact that people are living longer these days, that number is probably closer to $2 million today. And that number will continue to grow larger as you approach retirement age.

Many financial experts recommend that, in order to maintain the same level of comfort you are accustomed to now in your retirement years, you should aim to have at least the equivalent of 75 percent of you annual salary *(based on your last few years of employment)* available for each year of your retirement. However, this recommendation fails to account for a number of factors, like inflation, medical costs, life-changing events – such as disability or ill health – as well as the lifestyle you want to lead during your retirement years.

So what is the right answer? Only you can answer that question. For example, if you want to retire when reach the age of 45 so you can sail around the world in your personal yacht with a white-coated crew of 20, you had better start investing every spare cent you have, and hope you choose the correct retirement investments that offer unheard of returns. However, if your idea of retirement is enjoying a comfortable life of relaxing in the backyard with your grandkids, you can take a more conservative approach to investing for your retirement.

As you can see, determining how much money you need to retire involves a lot of personal decisions. It also involves a lot of financial decisions – primarily how you will invest your money to reach your retirement goals.

Defined-Benefit vs. Employer-Sponsored Plans

Your employer may give you the option to participate in one of two types of retirement plans. These include:

Defined-Benefit Plans

Defined-benefit plans are commonly referred to as pension plans. These types of plans were very common when your grandparents were your age – when employees worked for the same company for 20 to 30 years. These plans provide a guaranteed lifetime income during retirement. Benefits at retirement vary depending on how long you were with the company, how much you earned, and how old you are when you opt to retire. The funds are commingled – which means all employees' monies are kept in the same pot, and your employer manages that pot. It is important to note that this form of retirement planning is disappearing quickly from the corporate landscape. In addition to the fact that employees are no longer working for the same company for 20-plus years, corporate abuses and a volatile stock market have put these plans in bad graces in recent years. As a result, it is highly unlikely that you will see this type of plan offered during your employment years.

Employer-Sponsored Plans

Examples of employer-sponsored plans include 401(k), 403(b) and 457 plans. Unlike defined-benefit plans, these plans do not guarantee a specific payout amount upon retirement. Your payout depends on several factors: how much you and, possibly, your employers contributed over the years, and how well the investments did. Your retirement account is your own and no one else's money is commingled. You make the decisions on how the money is to be invested from many options, such as mutual funds, annuities, money-market funds or your company's stock, usually offered to you in package options by your employer. One of the best benefits of these plans is that you can take them with you when you change employers.

Employer-Sponsored Plans

As just mentioned, many employers now offer their employees the option to participate in employer-sponsored retirement plans. If your employer has one, do not pass up the opportunity to participate. There are real incentives for participation:

- Contributions are tax free, and the earnings in your account are untaxed until you retire and begin to take the money out.
- In 2005, you can contribute as much as $14,000. This number will increase to $15,000 in 2006. After 2006, annual contribution limits are expected to continue to rise.
- Your contributions can be handled automatically by payroll deduction, so you don't "feel" the loss.
- Most of these plans have no fees attached.

- Some employers even contribute to your plan.
- You will earn compounded interest on your contributions.

401(k) Plans

The 401(k) plan, offered by private companies, is a sweet deal for the employee. The tax savings can be significant to you. Here's how the deductions work: if you contribute $200 a month, or $2,400 a year, and you are in the 28 percent tax bracket, you can deduct the entire $2,400 off your gross income before your taxes are figured. That will put some $672 back in your pocket at tax time. In other words, the $2,400 contribution to your own account only costs you $1,728. In some states, 401(k) contributions are also tax-deferred on your state tax returns, and that will save you an additional 5 or 6 percent, depending on your state income tax bracket. Your investments grow untaxed, and you save money to boot. Don't pass this one up.

403(b) and 457 Plans

403(b) and 457 plans are quite similar to 401(k) plans, except that they are offered outside of the private sector. 403(b) plans are offered by non-profit, tax-exempt employers such as churches, hospitals, foundations and private schools. 457 plans are offered by federal, state and local government agencies and some non-profit organizations established by the government. These plans, like the 401(k), are defined-contribution, and your contributions and earnings are tax deductible up to set limits.

Employer Match Option

Another benefit of employer-sponsored plans is the employer match option. Here, the employer matches a certain, stated percentage of your contribution – typically between 50 and 100 percent – up to 6 percent of your annual gross salary. If your employer has a matching program, make every effort to maximize your own contribution. This really is free money! So be sure you take advantage of it.

Contribution Limits

As mentioned before, the tax benefits associated with employer-sponsored retirement plans are significant. However, there are limits on how much of this benefit you can take advantage of. With an employer-sponsored plan, you are likely to receive paperwork each year that keeps you apprised of the limits. Exceeding the limits has significant and unpleasant tax consequences, so be sure to keep abreast of these changes.

Vesting

Vesting refers to your ownership rights in your retirement money. You are always 100 percent vested in your own contributions, meaning that all money contributed by you from your own funds belongs to you at all times. However, if your employer provides matching funds, these funds often do not vest until a certain time period has elapsed. And even then, they will vest in incremental percentages set by the employer. This means that even though you are watching your retirement funds grow, if you leave that job before the stated number of years elapse, you must leave behind some or all of the corporate contribution. Following is an example of a traditional vesting schedule:

Sample Vesting Schedule

Years of Employment	Percent Vested
1	0%
2	20%
3	40%
4	60%
5	80%
6	100%

When considering a job change, pay close attention to your employer's vesting schedule, because it could wind up costing you a chunk of your future. Sometimes it makes more sense to stay in a job a bit longer than you'd otherwise consider doing in order to reach that golden moment when your retirement funds are fully vested.

Changing Jobs

Changing jobs is always an important consideration due to an increasing lack of job security. Whether or not your retirement plan is portable should make a big difference in your career planning. But here, again, the IRS has very specific rules and requirements as to how and where you move your plan. You have three options for moving your retirement money:

- If your account exceeds $5,000, you may opt to leave your money with your old employer, undisturbed, where it will continue to grow at a compounded rate.

- You may be allowed to roll your old retirement funds into your new employer's plan. Check the rules, and coordinate with the personnel office on this.

- You may set up your own plan through your broker, your bank, or with a mutual fund company.

If you do move your plan, be sure to touch all the bases. Skip one, and the financial penalties will shock you. It's not that hard, but you'd be wise to ask a professional, like your financial planner, a tax advisor, or a mutual fund company to help you do it by the book.

Self-Employed And Small Business Plans

So what if you're self-employed or work for a small business? What retirement options are available to you? It's true that you don't have the option of joining the large plans established and run by big corporations. However, there are several retirement plan options available to you.

Simplified Employee Pension (SEP)

A SEP is particularly good for someone who is self-employed and has no employees. Technically, only the employer can contribute to the plan. But if you are self-employed, you are the employer. Therefore, you can contribute up to 15 percent of your earnings, up to a maximum of $40,000 each year. This is deducted off the top of your income, offering you a sweet tax break – and even better if you live in a state that allows the deduction from your state taxes. These contributions can be made up to the day you file your return, but be scrupulously careful to make the contribution on time. The IRS does check, and if you have let the date slide, even by a day, it will be disallowed.

As an employee of a small business that participates in a SEP program, there is one major drawback – your employer has complete control of your contribution level. The maximum allowed is 15 percent of your salary, up to a maximum of $40,000. As usual, watch for changes to this number in the coming years.

Savings Incentive Match Plan (SIMPLE)

A SIMPLE is a plan that is offered by businesses that have no other kinds of plan offerings and have fewer than 100 employees. The key word here is "match." In a SIMPLE, the employee can contribute up to $10,000 annually, and the employer must match 100 percent of that contribution, up to 3 percent of your annual gross compensation. If you don't make your own contribution (*bad idea!*), the employer must contribute 2 percent of your salary, up to a maximum of $3,200. Your contribution, like the 401(k) and traditional IRA, is deductible, and the earnings in your account are tax deferred.

Keogh Plans

Keogh plans, also referred to as money-purchase or profit-sharing plans, are tax-deferred pension plans for those with self-employment income. Here are examples of Keogh plans:

- Money-purchase plans require the same contribution every year, even in years when you make no profit. Contributions are capped at $40,000, or 25 percent of your self-employment income, whichever is less.

- Profit-sharing plans are looser in requirements: contributions from 0 to 25 percent of self-employment income, up to $40,000, can be made each year. Keogh plans are complicated, paper-intensive, and not for the faint-of-heart, business-wise. It is best to use a financial professional to help you set up and maintain these.

Individual Retirement Accounts (IRAs)

If your employer doesn't offer a retirement program, or you wish to make additional retirement contributions, an IRA may be right for you. IRAs carry the same tax-deferral benefits as do the 401(k) and other employer-sponsored plans. However, the "individual" in the title means that these plans belong to you. Your employer has nothing to do with them. Following are descriptions of your IRA options.

Traditional IRA

This is a retirement plan created by you, and formally designated as such. You will usually work with a financial planner, bank, brokerage house or mutual fund company in setting up your IRA. It does not have to be terribly complicated, but it does require specific initial paperwork and precise annual documentation. In other words, you are not allowed to simply designate a certain portion of your regular account as retirement, and commingle other funds with it.

The traditional IRA can exist alongside an employee-sponsored plan, but there will be limits on the contribution levels if you are contributing to another plan. Contributions and earnings are tax deductible, provided you meet certain criteria:

- If you are single and are not participating in an employer-sponsored plan, you can put up to $4,000 a year into your IRA and deduct the full amount on your tax return.

- If you are single and are covered by an employer-sponsored plan, and your annual adjusted gross income is $30,000 or less, you can contribute up to $4,000 and deduct the whole amount. If your income is between $30,000 and $40,000, your deduction will be prorated. If your income is $40,000 or higher, you may contribute to the plan, but you will not be eligible for the tax deduction.

- If you are married, filing jointly, have an employer-sponsored plan, and your annual adjusted gross income is $50,000 or less, you can deduct the full amount of your $4,000 contribution. Deductions are prorated if your income is between $50,000 and $60,000.

- If you are married, file jointly, and your spouse does not have an employer-sponsored plan, your spouse can deduct the full $4,000 contribution up to $150,000 in joint income. The deduction is prorated up to $160,000, with no deduction allowed past that.

Note, that contribution levels and eligibility requirements change year to year. Check with the IRS at www.irs.gov for the most current information. In addition, even if your contribution is not tax deductible under any of these scenarios, there is still a substantial benefit to making the maximum contribution anyway – first, because your goal is to save as much as you can for retirement; and second, because the earnings from the IRA account are tax deferred, which means you do not pay taxes on these earnings until you retire and begin to withdraw the cash.

Roth IRA
The Roth IRA differs from the traditional IRA in several significant ways. The major difference is that your initial contribution is not tax deductible, unlike the traditional IRA, but withdrawals after retirement are not taxable, as they are with other plans. This can be very appealing in your later years.

Another difference is that if you've held the Roth IRA for at least 5 years and have reached the age of 59.5, you can withdraw your money without penalty, which can be a great way to tap into your investment if you must. Early withdrawals from traditional IRAs result in substantial penalties and back taxes. Moreover, you are not required to take your money out when you reach the age of 70.5, as you must with traditional IRAs. If you are so inclined, you can even leave the money, tax-free, to your heirs. Note, however, that if you are single and your income exceeds $110,000, or you are married and your income exceeds $160,000, you are not eligible for a Roth IRA. As usual, these numbers will change, so keep your eye on eligibility requirements.

Which Option *(Traditional vs. Roth IRA)* Is Best For You?
The answer to this question requires a careful analysis of your personal circumstances. The upfront tax deductions you are entitled to from a traditional IRA are pretty appealing, because they enable you to maximize your contributions with less squeeze on your current income. But, on the flip side, the tax-free payouts you're entitled to after retirement with the Roth IRA are just as appealing.

You need to think through what your financial position is likely to be in your retirement years, and that means weighing your current job posture, your lifestyle, your spending habits, your and your dependents' health and—this one is a real roll of the dice—where the economy is likely to be by then. Yes, your spending will decrease when you are older—perhaps your mortgage will be paid off, for example—but, at the same time, your medical expenses are likely to go way up, inflation will have increased costs, and you might be in the mood to take some of those nice trips you've been putting off all those years you were tied to your desk.

With so many variables, and no crystal ball, it's hard to know exactly what your retirement needs will be. So, if the present tax deduction is important to your making ends meet and making the maximum IRA contribution, by all mean go with a traditional IRA. But if you are disciplined and have a few bucks left over at the end of each pay period, give some thought to going with the Roth IRA, provided you live up to your obligation to yourself and your family and make those contributions on time. But, if you fall into the categories discussed above that preclude you from deducting a traditional IRA contribution because of income limits or marital status, the Roth IRA is the sensible way to go.

Social Security

Social Security was created as a federal program in 1935, when America was in the depths of the Great Depression. It was designed to supplement people's retirement savings, not to replace them. Too many people over the years have made the fatal mistake of thinking that Social Security was the only retirement plan they needed. Even now, with cost of living increases over the years, the Social Security benefit can be as little as a few hundred dollars a month, depending on how much you have contributed into the system over the years. Even if you max out on how much Social Security will pay, you are unlikely to come anywhere near your last annual earnings before retirement. And that's the good news.

The bad news is that the system is broken, and all but broke financially. In 1940 there were 42 workers contributing into the fund for every one retiree. By 1950 the ratio was 16.5 to one. The present ratio is about 3.3 to one. The oldest baby boomers are beginning to retire now, and by 2030 the ratio of workers to retirees is projected to be 2 to one, which will be impossible to sustain. Retirees will either have to be paid out of current government revenues, benefits will have to be slashed, or both.

The government has already had to do some major tweaking by raising the age at which one can begin to collect benefits, from 65 to 66 at present. This was politically unpopular, but necessary. Look for the age to rise again when the baby boomers begin clogging the system, well before you retire. More dramatic changes are in the works to keep the program alive.

The moral of the Social Security story: do not factor in Social Security when doing your retirement planning. If it's still there when you retire, think of it as an unexpected gift from the government.

Although the Social Security system does have its problems, it is a good idea to have an idea of where you stand on Social Security, because the program does offer disability and survivor benefits to your family in a worst-case scenario. The Department of Labor will provide you with a free copy of your Personal Earnings and Benefit Statement (PEBES), which will show your earnings through your last tax return, and what you can expect in benefits under various options. Call 800-772-1213 to receive your statement, or you may order it online at www.ssa.gov.

Seven Steps To A Successful Retirement Program

We've given you the basics. Now, how do you go about making all this work?

1. Start participating now!
If there is one point you should have picked up from this chapter, it's that now is the time to start participating in a retirement plan. Not next year, not next month, now. Retirement comes upon you much faster than you realize, and you cannot afford to give up the allure of compounding interest by failing to get into and contributing faithfully to a plan.

2. Make your contributions automatic.
Whatever plan you have picked, try to set it up so that an automatic contribution comes out of each paycheck—the same amount each pay period. This will make the process of funding your retirement much easier, and soon you won't even realize that the money is missing from your wallet. If you work for a company, even a small one, it should be easy to set this up with the office manager or personnel office. If you have set up your own plan, try to arrange for an automatic draft from your bank account, either monthly or quarterly.

3. Choose an asset allocation plan you can live with.
An asset allocation, or balanced, portfolio takes much of the guesswork and luck out of investing. You want the right mix of low and high-risk investments, a well-balanced selection of stocks, bonds, and cash equivalents. See the Investing chapter for more information on this subject.

4. Avoid early withdrawals and cash-outs.
During lean times it can be tempting to take a little of your retirement money to get by, but do all you can to avoid that temptation. Not only will you lose the benefit of your hard-earned savings, as well as the compounded interest that would have accrued, but early withdrawal penalties can be substantial. Remember that it is likely that this money

was not taxed at the time of your contribution, so the IRS will insist on recouping that tax. Plus, as a real disincentive, you will likely pay a 10 percent penalty on whatever you take out. This is enough to erode any benefit you received on your investments to date.

5. Avoid borrowing against your retirement plans.

Most 401(k) plans have a loan feature that allows you to borrow certain amounts from your account. Generally you must repay the loan within five years or less, at an interest rate set by the plan administrator. But you should make every effort not to resort to this, for the same reasons mentioned in the section above.

6. Avoid retirement plans with hefty fees.

Fees come in all shapes and sizes. Some are called administrative fees, some are called service fees, and some are called investment fees. You can't expect these plans to be administered for free, of course, but it will pay to learn what plans come with what fees, and to get that information you may have to comb the fine print. Choose the plan that gives you the features and services you want, and don't pay fees for something you don't need if you can help it.

7. Review your plan annually.

Retirement plans are definitely a long-term proposition. And things change—your personal circumstances, your job, rules about contributions and tax consequences. Retirement planning is an ongoing activity, and not something you want to fall behind on. Note, as well, that there are ups and downs in the market—that's a given—and you should not follow your portfolio every day and make rash decisions based on a few days' performance. Use your annual review to make sure your asset allocations are meeting your goals.

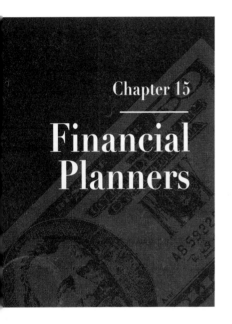

Chapter 15

Financial Planners

If you don't know where you're going, how are you ever going to get to your destination? You won't. This is especially true for financial planning. Do you need a plan? Absolutely. Do you need to hire a professional financial planner? It depends on you. For example, what is you level of comfort with financial matters? How much time do you have to do your planning? And what is your willingness to learn? Obviously, you have a willingness to learn. After all, you are reading this book.

If you aren't sure you can handle such a weighty responsibility and would be comfortable with some coaching from a professional, then a financial planner may be the way to go. But keep in mind, in the end you are going to be the best financial planner you have.

What Makes Someone A Good Financial "Coach"?

If you decide you need some financial advice, a financial planner is an excellent resource to use. However, you don't want just any financial planner. You want a financial planner who will be your financial "coach." What does this mean?

- Coaches understand, help, advise, sympathize, and praise. A financial coach will want to know everything there is to know about your financial situation, not just how much money you have to invest. A good coach will ask: What are your financial goals?

- A good coach will ask: What financial problems do you have (*debt, bad credit, lack of insurance, etc.*)?

- A good coach will ask: What assets and liabilities do you have?

In addition, your coach should:

- Help you set priorities.
- Provide an objective voice.
- Mediate between you and your spouse or life partner if need be.
- Help develop a strategy and review it regularly with you.

If the financial planner you are considering can't do all or most of these, keep looking for one that can.

How Do Financial Planners Earn A Living?

Financial planners don't give you financial advice simply to feel good about themselves. They do it to earn an income. Therefore, you need to be very clear about how your financial planner is being paid. There are basically four ways financial planners make money:

Through Commissions
These people aren't really financial planners at all – they're more like salespeople that are paid a commission on everything they sell. If this strikes you as a bit of a conflict of interest, you're absolutely right. Think about this another way: Say you're in the market for a new computer and you call a Dell Computer representative for advice. You wouldn't expect the Dell Computer representative to recommend that you purchase an Apple computer just because it better meets your needs.

Through Fees
Fee-based planners charge a percentage of the assets they are helping you manage. The bigger the assets, the more they make. But fee-based planners are generally only interested in people who have a large chunk of money to start with. In fact, some planners won't even take on clients who don't meet a minimum asset threshold.

Through a Combination of Commissions and Fees
Some planners charge to develop a plan for you, and then collect commissions by selling you the things the plan says you should buy. But there are pitfalls here as well. Imagine buying a car from a dealer – we'll call him a Transportation Consultant – who gets a fee for selling the car and then gets a commission on every gallon of gas you put into it. Does this seem like a good deal?

Through Fees Only
These planners charge by the hour, or offer a flat rate to develop a plan for you. The problem is that when you want to implement your plan, you'll

need to either do it yourself or pay for additional help. These types of planners tend to be the least biased. If you're comfortable with executing the plan on your own with the advice they have provided you, this may be the way to go.

Where Can You Find A Financial Coach?

There are a number of resources you can use to find a financial coach. These include:

Networking
The best way to find such a person is to ask – your friends, your boss, your family. If you know someone who is financially stable, ask who helps him or her with their financial planning.

Researching On Your Own
There are a number of places to find basic information on financial planners:

- **The Internet** – Check out the Financial Planning Association Web site www.fpanet.org, the National Association of Personal Financial Advisors www.napfa.org, or the Certified Financial Planner Web site www.cfp-board.org.
- **The Phone Book** – Look under Financial Planners and/or Financial Consultants. You should find a list of nationally recognized firms (like Fidelity, Smith Barney, and American Express Financial Advisors) and local firms that specialize in financial planning.
- **Your Bank** – In recent years, banks have expanded the services they offer to include financial planning. Ask your bank whether they offer this service.

Interviewing A Prospective Coach

Regardless of how you find prospective financial coaches, you need to make sure they are the right person for the job. How do you do this? Choose the top few candidates and interview them. Questions you should ask include:

- How do you charge for your services (*commissions, hourly, etc.*)?
- Do you perform other services, like tax advice or legal services?
- What qualifies you to be my financial coach?
- How long have you been a financial planner?
- How many clients do you have? How big is the asset base you manage for those clients?

- What kind of liability insurance do you carry?
- Can you give me references?
- If I hire you, will I be able to implement the financial strategy on my own?
- Once the plan is complete, how is implementation accomplished?

Go into the interview prepared to spend a couple of hours. Don't be shy about asking these questions and taking notes. You'll need to compare the results from each of your interviews before you make your hiring decision.

What About Certifications?

In your search for a financial coach, you probably noticed many financial planners have certifications after their names and titles. These certifications are awarded either by private organizations or industry associations and, while they require some experience or training, none is recognized by state or federal government entities. Therefore, take certifications and titles with a grain of salt.

One certification that does carry some value is provided by the Certified Financial Planner Board of Standards, which designates planners as a Certified Financial Planner (CFP). These individuals must pass a stringent examination process, meet specific experience requirements, as well as adhere to a strict code of ethics. In addition, if you plan to seek out advice from your financial planner on purchasing securities, such as stocks and bonds, be sure your planner has passed the National Association of Securities Dealers, Inc.'s (NASD) exam.

Things Your Financial Planner Should Never Do

Most financial planners are good people who give solid financial advice. However, there are some who are only in the financial planning service as a means to take advantage of their customers. Always be cautious of the information you provide a financial advisor, and always ask questions if you are ever unsure about their request. Here's a list of things a financial planner should never do:

- Ask you to make checks out to him or her personally – except to pay fees. Checks for investments should be in the name of the brokerage firm or mutual fund.
- List himself as a joint owner on any accounts.
- List himself as a beneficiary on any of your accounts.

- Ask you to lend him money. If he needs to borrow money, he's not doing his job well.
- Ask for discretionary authority over your accounts. Discretionary authority gives your planner the ability to buy and sell without asking you first. This is especially dangerous if your planner works on commission.
- He signs your name to documents.
- Ask you to sign a blank form or contract. Always cross-out any sections on the form that don't apply or fill the blanks with N/A.
- Put his address on your account statements. Statements of account activity need to be sent to your mailbox, not your planner's.
- Offer to sell you something that you can buy only from him.
- Share your profits.
- Assign your agreement to another planner. If your planner retires, or otherwise leaves the business, your agreement with that person or their firm is over.
- Not contact you on a regular basis. The relationship you want with a financial planner is long-term. If yours only calls when there's money to be put into his pocket, look for a new planner – this isn't the relationship you want or need.

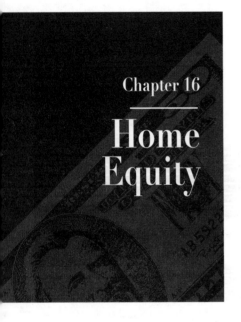

Chapter 16

Home Equity

Being the successful, financially savvy college graduate you are, the probability that you will own a home of your own is great. In addition, the chances are good that your home will offer a financial resource you can tap into if you need it. That financial resource is your home's equity – the value of your home minus the balance on your mortgage.

Home euity loans and credit lines seem to be popping up everywhere these days, and the terms can be quite tempting. While this is a legitimate and appropriate tool for putting your equity to work, it is crucial that you understand that, unlike credit card debt, which is unsecured, home equity loans and lines of credit are secured by your home. This means that you can lose your home if you fail to make payments. And your reasons for defaulting on your loan are irrelevant. It won't matter if you are ill or have lost your job – fail to make payments for any reason and you'll be out on the street with a suitcase.

That said, if you need to tap into your home equity, and if you do the right research and personal financial analysis, a home equity loan may be a good option for you.

Home Equity Loan vs. Line of Credit

These are two different animals, and understanding the difference is important.

Home Equity Loan (aka: Second Mortgage)
- Paid out as a flat sum.
- Structured like a traditional mortgage, with a fixed interest rate.
- Monthly payments are fixed and predictable.

Home Equity Line of Credit

- Allows you to withdraw money from your credit line whenever you want.

- Features a pre-approved limit based on your credit-worthiness and the amount of equity you have in your house.

- Most come with variable interest rates.

- You only pay interest on the amount of money you borrow.

- You may pay off all or part of the loan at any time, and re-borrow it when you wish.

- You draw on the credit line by using either specially issued checks or a credit card.

Which Option *(Home Equity vs. Line of Credit)* Is Best for You?

Generally, a home equity loan is best used to fund a specific project, like a home improvement project that has a plan, a budget and an anticipated start and end date. A line of credit is useful when your needs are ongoing but sporadic, like tuition or medical payments. In most instances, the line of credit can be cheaper since you only use what you need when you need it. But, as mentioned before, the interest rate will likely be variable.

What Can Home Equity Be Used For?

Legally, home equity can be used for anything your heart desires. But because this loan is secured by your home, it makes sense to have a very prudent, conservative plan for this money. While a big check or open line of credit may look like "free money" it is crucial that you treat it like what it is: a stake in your home.

The smartest use of your home equity is to improve your long-term financial posture. Following are some wise and not-so-wise methods for using your home's equity.

One of the real advantages of a home equity loan or credit line over other types of consumer debt is its potential deductibility. While credit card and automotive debt are not deductible on your tax returns, home equity loans – like traditional mortgages – may be deductible in amounts up to $100,000. This means you can subtract whatever interest you pay in any calendar year from that year's income. If you use the loan proceeds specifically for home improvements, you can deduct the interest on a loan up to $1 million. Do the math on the impact to your tax bill. This may put some serious cash back into your pocket.

Home Improvement Projects

A home equity loan used for home improvement, repairs or upgrades will likely increase your home equity. When used wisely, a home equity loan can actually increase your home equity by increasing the market value of your home. For example, updating kitchens and bathrooms are often a wise use of resources, while adding a pool or sauna may not add as much value as the work costs. Basic maintenance, such as installing a new roof, does not add value, but may prevent a decrease in value. Check with licensed real estate professionals in your area before you determine how to spend your home improvement dollars.

Debt Consolidation

Consolidating all of your debts under a home equity loan can make your credit debt more affordable and manageable, not to mention possibly tax deductible. Credit card debt at high interest rates can be consolidated into one debt at a lower interest rate. Student loans, as well, may be paid off and rolled into your home equity line. But check the interest rate, the payoff rate, and the deductibility of your student loan before making that move.

WARNING!!!

It makes no sense whatsoever to consolidate your credit card debt if you are just going to go out and run up more debt. If your spending is consistently more than your monthly income, you need serious credit counseling, not more credit.

Education

Using your home's equity to invest in your future or the future of your children is among the wisest moves. Education will improve your or your children's employment opportunities and salary levels for the long-term, and is money well spent.

Major Purchases

Using a home equity loan to purchase a car, boat, vacation or other big-ticket item is not wise. Nothing you buy for fun is worth risking your house. Of course, if you have an existing loan at a higher interest rate and can save money by rolling it into a home equity loan then, by all means, do so. Just do the math first and be sure of your numbers.

Living Expenses

The worst use of your home's equity is to cover your living expenses. If you are living above your means, seek professional help. The last thing you need is to be in over your head in debt and homeless.

Emergencies

Life can hand us some tough, unexpected situations. An open line of credit can be a lifesaver if you get laid off, encounter medical problems, or need to help out a family member. None of these uses builds value for you, of course, but difficult times call for tough measures. If you must tap into your home equity for an emergency, do your best to keep a close eye on your spending, cut back where you can, and pay back your loan as soon as you feasibly can do so.

When you apply for a home equity loan, as opposed to a line of credit, the lender will almost always want to know what you intend to do with the proceeds. If the lender feels your plan is too risky, your loan request likely will be rejected.

Is Using Home Equity Right for You?

Just because there's a pot of money available to you doesn't mean you have to use it. If you do use your home equity to consolidate other loans, make every effort to pay off the new note at the same or faster rate than the old debt. Your goal should always be to pay off your debt, not increase it. If you are the personality type who can't let a dollar sit unspent, avoid the lure of your home equity or line of credit.

Tax Deductibility

The tax deductibility factor is crucial to your decision-making. Get out your calculator and run the numbers. While tax deductions are enticing, they may be offset by other considerations such as the fees associated with obtaining a home equity loan or line of credit, which can be substantial. It pays to shop around.

- Your own bank may offer you a home equity loan at a slightly better rate than it would offer a non-customer.

- Consult a professional. Your financial planner or realty broker may have suggestions.

- Fees charged by the lender can include origination fees, appraisals, points, pre-payment penalties and any other charges that lenders can think up.

- While these fees can add up to hundreds, if not thousands, of dollars, they vary greatly from one lending institution to the next.

- It makes no sense to consolidate credit card loans at a slightly lower interest rate if the fees more than offset the savings.

Fees and Penalties

Check into lender policies on late fees and penalties and be sure you understand what they are and how they are assessed. They may look like just a few dollars here and there each month, but over a few years' time they can eat away at your assets. Also, if the lender mentions in very small print that it will jack up your variable interest rate the morning after you are late with a payment, go to another lender.

Length of Ownership

A final, but important, consideration is the length of time you plan to stay in your present home. All home equity loans or lines of credit fall due in full upon sale of your home. A home equity loan that has a pre-payment penalty may not be cost-effective if you plan to sell your home in a year. Likewise, the up-front fees you pay to obtain the loan need some time to be amortized before you can start seeing real savings.

The 125 Percent Home Equity Loan

How fast can you run? Good, because you should avoid this deal at all costs. What is it? Basically, these deals aren't home equity loans at all. They are a total refinancing of your first mortgage, allowing you to borrow up to 125 percent of the value of your home.

These loans use the Loan-To-Value (LTV) calculation, which is the ratio between what you owe on your house and what it's worth. In times past, lenders did not think it fair or safe to lend more than 80 percent of a home's value. Gradually, that number crept up to 90 percent. Now it seems anything goes, with lenders ready to hand out up to 125 percent of a home's value. This is dangerous to you for several reasons:

- These loans usually come with a hefty price tag in the form of high interest rates.

- You cannot deduct any interest paid on the loan over 100 percent of the value, which makes them even more expensive.

- If you have to move for an unexpected reason, you will have to pay off the loan or line of credit.

- If you want to buy a new house, you'll have next to nothing to use as a down payment.

- Even if you don't have to sell, it can take many years to pay down such a big note. You'll feel like you're deep in a hole you can't climb out of, and you'll be right.

The only time it is wise to take on a 125 percent loan is if you plan to do a carefully researched and well thought-out home improvement that is virtually guaranteed to add substantial value to your home. And even then you'd be wise to think twice.

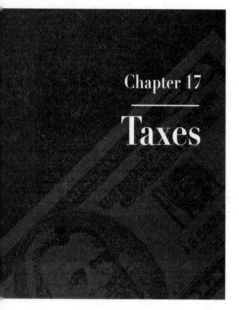

Chapter 17

Taxes

As the great Benjamin Franklin once said, "In this world nothing can be said to be certain, except death and taxes." How true he was.

Everyone pays taxes. However, do you know how much tax you are paying each year or how that money is being spent? Unfortunately, very few people truly know the answers to these questions. All they seem to remember is if they got a refund or if they owed money.

Think about paying your taxes in a different context. Lets say every payday a person shows up at your house and demands 30 to 40 percent of your paycheck. Wouldn't you want to know who keeps sending this person to collect money from you, how this person determines how much of your money should be taken, and what your money is being used for? Sure you would. This chapter will answer all these questions and more.

By reading this chapter, you will, in effect, become an informed and educated taxpayer. Will reading this chapter help you get out of paying taxes? No. Will reading this chapter help you reduce your taxes? Possibly. Will reading this chapter help you have a voice in how your tax dollars are spent? Definitely.

Understanding Taxes

To develop a better understanding of taxes, you need to consider the answers to the following questions.

Why Do We Pay Taxes?

As you may recall from the U.S. Government class you took way back when, the role of our government is to provide for our defense, regulate commerce, establish justice, insure domestic tranquility, and promote the general welfare. To accomplish these tasks, the government requires funding. This funding is generated by the taxes you pay. You might say that taxes are the price we pay to live in a civilized society.

What Kind Of Taxes Do We Pay?
You pay taxes on a lot of different things. Some you may be familiar with, and others you may not. Following is a list of the most common taxes you pay.

- **Income Tax** – is a tax on your income. In addition to the federal government, some state and local governments also require you to pay a tax on your income.

- **Sales Tax** – is a tax on the stuff you buy and the services you use.

- **Property Tax** – is a tax on applicable property. A home is the most common. However, some states and local governments also apply property taxes to other forms of property, like a car, boat or recreational vehicle.

- **Social Security and Medicare Tax** – commonly referred to as FICA, which means the Federal Insurance Contributions Act, is a tax used to fund retirement income and health insurance to people 65 and over. In most cases you pay half of this tax and your employer is required to pay the other half. However, if you are self-employed, you are required to pay the entire amount. This is commonly referred to as the Self-Employment Tax.

Who Creates The Taxes You Pay?
When asked who creates the taxes you pay, most people answer the Internal Revenue Service (IRS). However, this is incorrect. The correct answer is the politicians who make up our government.

Politicians are always quick to pass the blame for unpopular issues, like taxes, to someone else. But when you look back at every tax law on the books today, they all started as an idea thought up and voted into law by politicians.

Once the politicians pass a tax law, it is forwarded to the Department of the Treasury. There, they develop regulations on how the tax will be imposed, collected, etc. After that process is completed, the regulations are forwarded to the IRS *(a bureau of the Department of Treasury)*. The IRS is then given the unpleasant task of enforcing the tax law.

Who Decides How Your Tax Dollars Are Spent?
Ultimately, it's you. Yes, that's right, you decide. You do this by choosing the representative *(politician)* who will represent your interests in our government.

We've all heard the horror stories of wasteful or unnecessary spending, commonly referred to as "pork barrel spending." For example, the government recently authorized $10 million of your tax dollars for additions to the Palace of Governors museum in Santa Fe, N.M. Wouldn't you rather have that money be used for new additions to your own house or, if you don't own a home, buy one for you? Or better yet, wouldn't you rather that money be used to create jobs for the unemployed or even reduce the governments overwhelming debt?

If you are unhappy with the level of taxation in your life, or you think your tax dollars can be better spent on more useful projects, then get involved. Understand where candidates for public office stand on taxes and how they believe those funds should be spent, and vote appropriately. Democracy isn't a spectator sport.

How Is Your Income Tax Calculated?

Unfortunately, there is no simple answer to explain how your income tax is calculated. It is an involved process that includes a number of variables, including your filing status, your taxable income, and your applicable income tax brackets. To assist you in understanding this process, each of these variables are explained in the following pages.

Filing Status

There are five different filing status groups. When you file your taxes you choose the group that most accurately describes your current situation. If your current situation makes you eligible for two of these groups, you should choose the one with the bigger deduction. The different groups include:

- **Single** – You are unmarried and do not qualify to file as Head of Household or Qualifying Widow(er).

- **Married, Filing Separately** – You are married as of the end of the tax year. You and your spouse each file a separate income tax return with your own income and deductions.

- **Married, Filing Jointly** – You combine your income and deductions with those of your spouse on the same tax return.

- **Head of Household** – You are not married and you maintain a household for an individual who qualifies as a dependent.

- **Qualifying Widow(er)** – You may be able to use this filing status for two years after the year your spouse died, allowing you to use the same rates as if you were filing jointly. To qualify, you must:

— Not remarry before the end of the tax year for which you are filing the return.

— Had the right to file a joint return in the year of your spouse's death.

— Have a dependent child living in your home and have paid more than half the cost of maintaining your home for that dependent. You may file a joint return with your deceased spouse for the year of your spouse's death. For two years thereafter, if all of these conditions are met, you can file using the Qualifying Widow(er) status.

Taxable Income

Determining your taxable income is a simple calculation. Unfortunately, the calculation involves a number of confusing terms. Therefore, before attempting the calculation, you should familiarize yourself with a few tax-related terms. These include:

- **Gross Income** – is all the taxable income you earned throughout the year. This includes earned income *(like wages, sick pay, and unemployment)* and unearned income *(like interest and dividends)*.

- **Adjustments** – are the amounts you can subtract from your gross income. This includes items like IRA contributions, alimony payments, and moving expenses.

- **Adjusted Gross Income (AGI)** – is your gross income minus adjustments.

- **Standard Deduction** – is a reduction to your AGI for you, your spouse, and your qualifying dependents. These amounts are established by the government.

- **Itemized Deduction** – is a reduction to your AGI for expenses like medical costs, mortgage interest, state and local taxes, employee business expenses, and charitable contributions.

- **Taxable Income** – is the amount of income used to calculate your income tax.

- **Credit** - is a direct dollar-for-dollar reduction of your income tax after it is computed on your taxable income. For example, the Child Tax Credit.

- **Witholding** – are taxes that are taken out of your wages or other income before you receive them and that are deposited in an IRS account.

- **Estimated Payment** – are quarterly tax payments you make to the IRS if your tax-withholding amount is inadequate. You may be required to make estimated tax payments if a significant amount of your income is not subject to withholding, such as net income from a business or investment income.

Now that you are familiar with these various tax-related terms, you are ready to calculate your taxable income, as well as your total income tax.

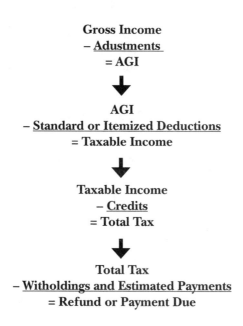

Gross Income
– Adustments
= AGI

↓

AGI
– Standard or Itemized Deductions
= Taxable Income

↓

Taxable Income
– Credits
= Total Tax

↓

Total Tax
– Witholdings and Estimated Payments
= Refund or Payment Due

Income Tax Brackets

In the previous calculation, you were able to determine how your total income tax is derived. However, the question of how much total income tax you owe still remains. How is that determined?

The United States uses a progressive tax system. With this system, taxable income levels are divided into brackets with lowest income brackets paying the least amount of tax. Tax brackets currently start at 10 percent and go to 35 percent. The more you earn, the more tax you pay. The chart provided below provides an excellent visual of the tax brackets used in 2004.

Filing Status and Income Tax Rates 2004

Tax rate	Married filing jointly or Qualified Widow(er)	Single	Head of household	Married filing separately
10%	$0 - 14,300	$0 - 7,150	$0 - $10,200	$0 - 7,150
15%	$14,301- 58,100	$7,151- 29,050	$10,201- 38,900	$7,151- 29,050
25%	$58,101- 117,250	$29,051- 70,350	$38,901- 100,500	$29,051- 58,625
28%	$117,251- 178,650	$70,351- 146,750	$100,501- 162,700	$58,626- 89,325
33%	$178,651- 319,100	$146,751- 319,100	$162,701- 319,100	$89,326- 159,550
35%	over $319,100	over $319,100	over $319,100	over $159,550

So how does the progressive tax system work? Lets pretend for a moment that you were single in 2004 and you had a total income of $51,550. After adjustments, deductions, and credits, you had a taxable income of $42,458. Here's how your taxes would be figured if you were filing as a single taxpayer:

Applicable Tax Brackets on $42,458	Tax Owed
10 percent tax on the first $7,150	$715
15 percent tax on the next $21,900	$3,285
25 percent tax on the last $13,408	$3,352
Total Tax Owed	**$7,352**

Marginal & Effective Tax Rates

At some time in your life you may have heard the terms marginal and effective tax rates thrown around, and wondered to yourself, "What are these and what do they mean to me?" Those are excellent questions.

Marginal Tax Rate – is the rate applied on your last dollar of earnings. In the previous example, the marginal tax rate is 25 percent. Knowing your marginal rate will help you evaluate the value of making certain investment decisions. This will be discussed in more detail in the Investing chapter.

Effective Tax Rate – is the rate calculated by dividing the total tax paid by your total income. In the previous example, the total tax paid is $7,352 and the total income is $51,550. Therefore, the effective tax rate is 14 percent. Knowing your effective tax rate will also help you evaluate the value of making certain investment decisions, but for the most part, the effective tax rate is used simply to determine your overall tax burden.

Reporting Your Taxes

Most people dread filing taxes, but if you go into the task prepared, it shouldn't cause much anguish. The first question is which of the four forms – 1040EZ, 1040A, 1040, and 1040PC – should you use? That will depend on your filing status, your income and the deductions and credits you have.

- **1040EZ** – Use this form if you are single, or married and filing jointly; have taxable income less than $100,000 and no itemized deductions.

- **1040A** – Use this form if you have income from several sources and your total income is less than $100,000. This form does not allow you to itemize, but does permit you to claim tax credits and take deductions for deductible IRA contributions and student loan interest.

- **1040** – Use this form if your itemized deductions are larger than the standard deduction, you receive income from a rental property or capital gains, or you own a small business.

- **1040PC** – Use this form if you wish to file your taxes online. Be sure the tax-preparation software you use is approved by the IRS.

If you filed a return last year, the IRS will happily send you a packet this year with the same form already in it. In most cases, unless your status has changed, *(you got a better paying job, got married, bought a house)* you can continue to use the form they send.

Because tax law changes frequently, you should check with the IRS www.irs.gov to be sure you choose the correct form. Taxes are incredibly complex and so are the regulations that go with them. The IRS has a wealth of information on their Web site to help you.

Reducing Your Tax Burden

Regardless of your income level, you should consider creating a plan to take advantage of tax breaks written into the tax code. This is all legal and above-board. And there are a number of sound ways you can use the tax laws to keep more of your income.

Tax-Exempt Investments – With some investments, notably the Roth IRA, any money you earn is tax-exempt – meaning you never have to pay taxes on it. Interest on Municipal Bonds is also generally tax-exempt._

Tax-Deferred Investments – Qualified 401(k) savings plans and IRAs allow you to make contributions, earn interest and dividends, but not pay the tax until you withdraw the money later in life. Theoretically, when you retire your tax bracket will be lower because you'll have less income, so any taxes you pay on money you withdraw from an IRA will be taxed at the lower rate. If you invest in securities that appreciate in value, you won't be taxed on that appreciation until and unless you sell those securities. Your $10 a share bargain that races to $65 a share is all profit on paper until you sell.

Home Equity Loans – Interest on most home equity loans, up to $100,000, is deductible. Interest on credit cards is not. Neither is interest on consumer loans. So, if you have credit card or consumer debt and equity in your home, you may want to consider taking out a home equity loan to pay down the debt – and deduct the interest from your gross income at tax time. Be sure that the home equity loan you apply for qualifies for tax a deduction before you sign anything.

Paying Expenses With Pre-Tax Dollars – Many employer health insurance plans offer flexible spending accounts *(see the Insurance chapter)* that allow you to use pre-tax dollars for health care. Money is deducted from your paycheck before your withholding tax is taken out, thus reducing the amount of money on which your tax is calculated.

Student Loan Interest – If you have student loans, interest paid during the year is deductible if the loan was used for tuition, fees, room and board, supplies and other related items, and certain income limits must are met. Because limits change from year to year, you should check the IRS Web site for current information to determine if you qualify.

Itemizing Deductions – Itemizing deductions can reduce your AGI. However, be aware that rules for applicable deductions change every year. So be sure to read the information that comes with your IRS Tax Return package. Examples of itemized deductions include:

- State and local taxes
- Points paid on your mortgage
- Charitable contributions
- Home office expenses
- Job search expenses
- Moving expenses – if they're related to a new job
- Gambling losses, but just up to the amount of gambling winnings

Keeping Records

Good record keeping habits will make tax preparation much easier. You should keep all records you used to prepare your tax return for at least three years. But keep that tax return itself forever – it may save you a lot of trouble later.

Here's a list of some of the kinds of records you should keep and for how long.

Type of Record	Keep It For
Annual Tax Return	Forever
Cancelled Checks, Bank Deposit Statements And Receipts	At least 3 years, 7 years is better
Stock Trade Confirmation Receipts/ Statements	At least 3 years after both the buy and sell transactions have closed
Home Improvements	At least 3 years after the sale of the property
Escrow Closing Documents	Minimum of 3 years after the property is sold
Tax Preparation Documents	3 years minimum

Tax Assistance

Resources are readily available to help you not only plan for your taxes, but prepare your return. You merely have to decide how much help you want. Following are some resources you might wish to consider.

IRS - The IRS www.irs.gov is the ultimate source of tax help. Their Web site is full of information to answer questions and direct you to helpful pages. If you prefer talking to a real person, a staff of IRS tax professionals is available to assist you by simply calling 800-829-1040.

Tax Publications & Web Sites – In addition to the useful publications produced by the IRS *(available in print or online)*, there are a number of books and Web sites available that offer solid advice. Do some research and you'll find a wealth of information to assist you.

Tax Preparation Software – The fastest-growing method of filing a tax return is electronically. The IRS encourages electronic filing, which is both fast and free if you use the Web. Benefits of filing electronically are speed of filing and faster refunds.

To file electronically, you will need to prepare your taxes with IRS approved tax preparation software – TurboTax and H & R Block's TaxCut are two of the more popular options. Advantages of using tax preparation software are:

- They are relatively inexpensive *(starting around $35)* and easy to use.
- You don't have to get forms; they're in the program.
- You can see what your tax liability is, and then make adjustments
- The software prompts you with questions to help you take advantage of possible tax reductions.
- If you enter the information correctly, there is minimal chance for errors.
- The program carries information over to and enters it in all the required places. Plus, it does all calculations.
- Carryovers from year to year are automatic, assuming you use the same program each year.

However, there are some disadvantages to using tax preparation software. First, and foremost, you have to trust the software. There's always a small chance that the software may have a flaw that can cause an error. In addition, if you're using an online service to file, there are always privacy concerns.

Be sure that the tax preparation software package you choose includes state income tax forms, if that applies to your state. Also, if you purchase the software early, remember to get an updated version so you have the latest information and tax-code revisions.

Professional Services

If you simply want to load up all your records and dump them on someone else there are a number of services available to assist you for a fee. These include Storefront Preparers *(like H&R Block and Jackson Hewitt Tax Services)*, Certified Public Accountants, Enrolled Agents, and Tax Attorneys.

Before you head off to seek help from one of these tax professionals, be sure you have done your research. Determine what you will be charged for these services. Fees can be as low as $50 to as high as $300 per hour. You will also want to locate a service that is qualified to assist you. The more difficult your taxes are to prepare, the more qualified the service provider should be. Finally, ask friends, family or coworkers to recommend specific tax professionals they have used.

Rapid Refund Offers

There are numerous tax preparation services offering customers "Rapid Refunds." Basically, this is a high-interest loan. You pay what appears to be a small fee, and in exchange your tax-preparer hands over your expected tax refund minus the fee.

Let's pretend for a moment that the IRS owed you $500. Instead of filing electronically and getting your money in two-weeks, you agree to pay a $34 fee for a "Rapid Refund." That rapid refund works out to an annual interest rate of over 200 percent. Yikes!!! And you thought an 18 percent interest rate on your credit card was bad.

If you are ever offered a "Rapid Refund," take your tax return and run. You're about to be robbed!

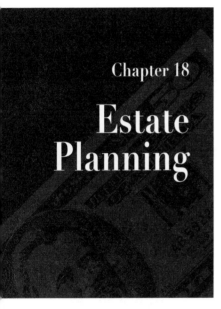

Chapter 18

Estate Planning

Nothing in life is truly predictable. Not in any great detail, anyway. However, one thing is for sure – you will die at some point. Hopefully in the far, distant future, but what if…? No matter what your age, you need to plan your estate.

What Is Estate Planning?

Your estate is what is left of your assets at the time of your death. Estate planning is the process of figuring out what you want done with your assets when you die, and drafting the documents that will make that happen. One reason to do estate planning is to minimize, legally, the taxes your estate has to pay the government. If you have a spouse and/or children, or others who are dependent on you, estate planning is a must. Even if your assets are thin at present, they will grow over the next few years. If you die without a will *(intestate, as it's called)*, your heirs, on top of dealing with their grief, will have to hire lawyers and accountants to straighten everything out.

What Is A Will?

A will is a legal document, drawn up according to specific state requirements, that is used upon your death to transfer your assets according to your stated wishes. Wills can be as simple or as complicated as your circumstances warrant, but they must be drafted properly and carefully.

Do I Need a Will?

The short answer to that question is yes. Everyone needs a will, even if he or she is unmarried and owns only a few assets. Having a will, properly and legally drawn up and executed, assures a smooth and tidy transfer of your assets to those whom you wish to benefit. If you die intestate, the state will decide who gets your assets and in what proportion – and that is often not a good thing. For example, if you are married with an infant and the unthinkable happens, your spouse may only get one-third to one-half of your estate, while the infant gets the rest. The court will then appoint a trustee to oversee the infant's share who may, or may not, be your spouse depending on who else wants to get into the mix.

What Should a Will Include?

- The will should list the dispositions of your personal property and other assets. Include the names of those you wish to benefit *(you may include businesses or charities)*, and in what amounts or proportions you wish your assets to be divided. Proportions do not have to be equal. You should further delineate how you wish less-easily divided property, such as a house, to be distributed.

- The will should name an executor, and possibly an alternate executor in case the first is unable to serve.

- The will should name a guardian if you have, or are planning to have, children. The guardian will be legally responsible for them until they are 18.

- If you have children under age 18, you will also need to set up a trust fund to see to it that their financial needs are met. In addition, you will need to name a trustee to manage the trust fund. This person may or may not be your childrens' guardian. You must also indicate the age at which the trustee turns the assets over to the children outright. If you say nothing on this point, your kids get everything at 18, which is an awfully young age to handle serious money.

- If you have children or heirs who have special needs, or who are not capable of managing their finances, you should make special arrangements in your will to address these circumstances.

What Is an Executor and Who Should This Person Be?

An executor is the person designated to carry out your wishes, and who interfaces with the court, and with creditors and heirs. The executor may not go against your stated wishes unless there is valid legal reason and, even then, the executor will have to explain the situation and ask for guidance from the court.

The executor initiates probate *(the process by which a will is legally certified to be valid)* by filing an application to appear before the probate court. The executor then presents the will to the court, which rules on its validity. This is a routine matter, unless the will appears invalid, or someone challenges it. After the will is authenticated, the executor takes inventory of the estate's assets, appraises the value of the assets, collects any amounts due to the estate, pays any bills owed by the estate, pays income and estate taxes as necessary, and then distributes the assets to the beneficiaries. After the assets have been distributed and all court costs paid, the executor applies to the court to finalize the estate and close it out.

The executor must be at least 18 and should be an honorable, organized, and reliable person. In addition, the executor will need to be a peacemaker and an authority figure, particularly if you believe there may be conflicts among family members and/or heirs when your executor carries our your wishes.

Medical Directive (aka: Living Will)

A medical directive, also known as a living will, is vitally important. A medical directive sets out in legal, enforceable terms what your desires are with regard to the kinds of life-sustaining and medical intervention you want in the event you become terminally ill and unable to communicate your wishes. Understand that if you do not have such a document, your relatives will make this decision for you. If there is dissension within your family on this point, the government and a whole host of activist groups will step in. It's your life and your death. Take control of it while you can.

What Is a Health-Care Power of Attorney?

A health-care power of attorney allows you to choose who you want to make medical decisions for you if you cannot make them yourself. To create a medical directive or living will, and a health-care power of attorney, you must be at least 18 years old and of sound mind. You must also be able to make and communicate medical decisions. You may appoint anyone who is at least 18 years old and competent, and who is not your health care provider, to be your health care agent. It is customary to appoint a spouse, parent or adult child, but you may appoint a friend or professional. It is wise to discuss this appointment with the person you choose before you make it final, and to be clear that this person does not have religious or social beliefs that conflict with what you want done. Once you have made this appointment, in the event of your incapacity, that person will have sole legal responsibility for carrying out your wishes.

What Is a Durable Power of Attorney?

A power of attorney is a document that legally authorizes a person to act as another's agent. Usually this is for a specific purpose, such as signing your name to a contract when you are out of the country, and ends at the completion of that purpose. "Durable" powers of attorney are designed to continue after a person becomes incompetent, and becomes effective when a person becomes incompetent. All powers of attorney end upon death.

In the event of your incapacity, you need to know that your affairs are being properly managed. It is wise to create a power of attorney so that your bills can be paid and your life kept in order. Not all incapacitating events end in death. If you are comatose for six months because of a bad automobile accident, if would be nice to wake up and not find that your home has been foreclosed on because no one had the ability to pay your mortgage. In spite of the name, the person you give power of attorney does not need to be an actual attorney. But as with your executor or trustee, you'll want someone who is honest, reliable, and well organized.

Probate And Trusts

Probate is the legal process that authenticates your will and oversees the disbursement of your assets according to your stated wishes after your death. Trusts are legal entities that are used to transfer some or all of the assets out of the estate for a specific reason, to be held by one person or entity for the benefit of another.

What Is Probate?

Probate is the process of validating the will, then implementing its terms, along with settling estate matters such as funeral costs and other expenses. Depending on the complexity of the estate, probate can take anywhere from six months to several years. Attorney expenses and court costs generally run about 3 to 5 percent of the estate. Very simple estates can be probated without an attorney, but legal help can save an executor from making costly mistakes for a medium-to-large estate. Not all assets go through probate. Life insurance benefits, which are designated to someone other than the estate itself, for example, fall outside of probate. So do 401(k) accounts, and assets owned jointly with another person. The more assets that legally can be kept out of probate, the lower the cost.

What Is a Trust?

A trust is a legal arrangement by which one person (a trustee) holds and manages money or property belonging to someone else. You might consider setting up a trust if you want your children to have the benefit of your assets, but your children are minors and cannot manage those assets themselves, or for some reason the person entitled to your trust is not in a position to receive the money outright. You can leave specific instructions as to how and when the trustee is to disburse the trust income to the beneficiary. Or you can leave the details up to the trustee.

Creating a trust is not a simple task. You must consult with a lawyer who practices specifically in that field – and don't expect him or her to work for peanuts. Under no circumstances should you buy a do-it-yourself trust kit, nor should you fall victim to high-pressure sales pitches pushing E-Z trust set up. This is a complex job that must be done right, for the sake of those you love.

Estate Taxes

"Death tax" is a popular term used in politics these days. However, there is no such thing as a death tax. You are not taxed for dying. There are estate taxes, but only a tiny minority of the country's wealthiest people pays these taxes. If you understand what estate taxes are, and plan appropriately, you can maximize what your heirs get.

What Are Estate Taxes?
Your estate consists of all your assets, including things that are excluded from probate, such as insurance proceeds and 401(k) funds. Stocks, bonds, jewelry, and insurance payouts – all items of value that belong to you are part of your estate when you die.

When you die, everything that you bequeath to your spouse is distributed tax-free. After that, the total amount of your remaining estate that you can pass tax-free to your heirs is scheduled to go up every year. In 2005, it will be $1.5 million. In 2006, it will be $2 million. It goes up to $3.5 million in 2009. The law is scheduled to expire in 2010, which would repeal all federal *(not state)* taxes, but it is not certain what Congress will do between now and then.

While these amounts may seem astronomical to you now, consider that with property values going up, and your investments earning compound interest, you may be a millionaire before you know it. When you reach the point in life when you start to look pretty prosperous on paper, it is time to bite the bullet and consult a reputable estate planner for advice on how to reduce a potential estate tax burden.

Do You Need An Attorney?

Well, as with so many complicated questions, that depends. If you are just starting out and your assets are slim, it doesn't make much sense to pay the expense of hiring an attorney to draft a simple will for you. There are many Web sites that offer free help in writing your own will, and the bookstore and library also have books to guide you. Before you plunk down hard-earned cash on an attorney, check out these resources.

But *(you knew that was coming)* things do change. If you die without a will, the state where you resided at the time of your death will have sole determination as to where your assets go. Once you have anything valuable, such as a house or a savings account, wouldn't you like to decide who should enjoy the fruits of your earthly labor? And the minute you get married or have offspring – or even better, as soon as you get engaged or are expecting a child – you need to get cracking on estate planning. And the best way to do that properly is to hire a knowledgeable attorney.

There are some important issues to consider here:

- Each state has a different set of complex requirements for drafting wills and estate planning. For example, some states will allow you to write a will in your own handwriting, but will discard it if there is other printing on the paper, such as a corporate logo or letterhead. In addition, all states have specific, stringent witnessing requirements. If you prepare your own estate plan, it might be wise to pay a small fee to have an attorney review your plan for omissions or possible errors.

- There is no fail-safe plan. Even if an attorney develops a plan for you, it can still be contested. Make sure that whatever is drafted is clear enough for the average layman to understand to minimize possible confusion as to what you meant.

- Do your homework and select a well-qualified professional to assist you. Check out the credentials of anyone you retain, and get references, if possible. Beware of "symposiums" and do-it-yourself plans.

- You don't want to re-draft your will every year. Plan for contingencies such as more children or the death of a parent, and make sure your will addresses these contingencies.

Funeral Arrangements

No one enjoys planning his or her own funeral, to state the obvious. However, a few well-chosen directives can save your grief-stricken heirs a great deal of angst that they surely won't need. Do not, under any circumstances, put your funeral instructions in your will. Death can be unexpected and dismaying for those you leave behind, and finding your will may be a task they are not up to at that moment. Funeral arrangements generally have to be made rather quickly, and there really isn't time to go scrambling around looking for a will. The best place to leave funeral directives is in a written document. You should store the original in your bank box, and store a copy in a file where you keep your home papers marked "Important." Be sure your spouse and/or family members know where to find this document.

As far as the actual arrangements, you should be clear on whether you want a religious service and, if so, pick the church or temple you prefer. Specify whether you want traditional burial or cremation and, if you want a burial, suggest a cemetery. If you have a real preference for what you want carved on your tombstone, be sure to spell it out. Otherwise, you are likely to spend eternity "Resting In Peace." Above all, give your heirs some idea of how much they should spend on a casket. There are a great many choices out there, ranging from the merely expensive to the obscenely outlandish, and you don't want a grief-stricken spouse being talked into the latter. The point is not to "take it with you," but to leave your loved ones as well off as possible, and go out with some degree of taste and dignity.